❦❦❦❦❦❦❦❦❦❦❦❦❦❦❦❦❦❦❦❦❦❦❦

Notes
Toward
A
New
Rhetoric

Notes
Toward
A
New
Rhetoric

SIX ESSAYS FOR TEACHERS

Francis Christensen
University of Southern California

HARPER & ROW, PUBLISHERS

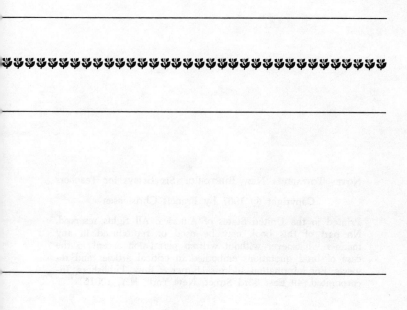

New Illustrated Title. Illustrations by the Translator.

Copyright © 1960 by Harper & Row

NEW YORK · EVANSTON · LONDON

NOTES TOWARD A NEW RHETORIC: Six Essays for Teachers

Copyright © 1967 by Francis Christensen

Library of Congress Catalog Card Number: 67–12553

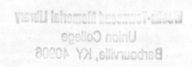

DEDICATION

To
My
Students
in
English 411b
and
401

Contents

❦❦❦ ❦❦❦❦❦ ❦❦❦❦ ❦❦❦❦❦❦❦

Preface

I cannot truly plead that in bringing these essays together I have been "obliged by hunger and request of friends." Yet some of them have been in request. Some have been included in collections of essays—a bit to stave off hunger there—and some, less formally, have been reproduced by ditto, mimeograph, and offset. This recognition has been gratifying, but many interested teachers have discovered only the two pieces that appeared in *College English*, others only those that appeared in 1963 or the one that came out in 1965. The pieces on the absolute and on nonrestrictive punctuation, dating back to the fifties, are probably not known to younger teachers at all. So it has seemed worthwhile to bring the six essays together in an order that shows their bearing on one another, with some connective tissue to relate them to one another and to the field of rhetoric and composition.[1]

They are reprinted by permission of the National Council of Teachers of English, with errors corrected but with few other changes except those required by transplanting from the pages of a journal. In two places I have avenged myself by restoring passages cut by editors who thought they were only hurting my pride and not my meaning. I have added postscripts to some of the essays to broaden their scope or deal with problems that were not apparent at the time of writing.

The hand-me-down rhetoric that we are trying to alter to fit the needs of our own times has three main divisions—invention, disposition, and style. These essays are concerned directly only with style, and yet not with the whole of style. To Swift, style was proper words in proper places. Although a good deal is implied about

---

[1]The six essays appeared as follows:

1. "In Defense of the Absolute," *College English* and *The English Journal*, May 1950.

2. "Restrictive and Nonrestrictive Modifiers Again," *College English*, October 1957.

3. "A Generative Rhetoric of the Sentence," *College Composition and Communication*, October 1963.

4. & 5. "Notes Toward a New Rhetoric: I. Sentence Openers; II. A Lesson from Hemingway," *College English*, October 1963.

6. "A Generative Rhetoric of the Paragraph," *College Composition and Communication*," October 1965.

proper words, the main concern in all the essays is with proper places—with the *structure* of the sentence and, beyond the sentence, with the *structure* of the paragraph. The rhetoric of the sentence and the paragraph has other concerns than structure, and to that extent these essays do not add up to a complete rhetoric even of the sentence and paragraph. But structure is fundamental.

In writing a piece of any length, one uses the resources of rhetoric in the order of their listing above—first invention, then disposition, and finally style. Although most rhetorics take up the divisions of their subject in this order, proceeding from the larger to the smaller units, it is an order that should not be allowed to dictate the order in which we take up these topics in teaching how to write. The longer the span of time for which a course or a curriculum is being planned, the more necessary it is to depart from this sequence in teaching. I believe that in the elementary school the writing should be self-expression, its goal simply fluency. Perhaps not until the sixth grade should we try to develop a sense of form and begin the long process of reconciling those perennial opposites, the inner and the outer worlds. To begin this discipline, and it is discipline, the best form of writing is narration and description, what we may call representational writing in contrast to discursive and persuasive. It is best because it is close to the child's experience; it is concrete and the problem of invention reduces itself to observation; because the content, sense impressions, is not already verbalized; because it is simple and can be further simplified by reducing it to its elements, as the first two essays show; because it can be limited in scope, to the scope actually of the sentence. In discursive writing, the paragraph is the natural unit, but in representational writing, it is the sentence. The idea of rhetoric as generative makes it possible to teach the sentence as professionals use it, and to teach it positively and creatively.

Still, we should not confuse means and ends. Narrations and descriptions, words and sentences, are means. The end is to enhance life—to give the self (the soul) body by wedding it to the world, to give the world life by wedding it to the soul. Or, more simply, to teach to see, for that, as Conrad maintained, is everything.

If we start discursive writing with the paragraph and if the student comes to the paragraph with the training in diction and sentence structure I have described, the start is an easy and natural one. The analogy between the structure of the sentence and the paragraph set up in the fourth essay makes it possible to talk sense about the paragraph.

Professor Kitzhaber has said that the first 500-word theme precipitates *all* the problems of writing. (The commander has to train the troops while the battle is going on.) This inundation is inevitable if we start with discursive writing, or restrict ourselves to it, and follow what seems the normal sequence of invention, disposition, and style. If we start with the smaller units, the student comes to the writing of long discursive essays already able to write. (The troops are already trained.) Then we can concentrate on what is peculiar to discursive writing—in invention, in disposition, in stance or voice. All these have to be funneled through the sentences and paragraphs; and the funnel is ready.

I want to make a special point of the fact that whatever is novel in the rhetorical principles advanced in these essays is based on close inductive study of contemporary American prose. Such induction is common enough in the study of usage (see Margaret M. Bryant, *Current American Usage*, 1962), though many English teachers call it nose counting and dismiss the results, preferring to abide by the prescriptions of the textbooks they were brought up on. This preference is one that I cannot understand, since it means taking the word of the amateurs who hack out textbooks that talk about language (fools like me) as against the practice of professionals who live by their skill in using language. In the second and third essays I have taken to nose counting in order to establish rhetorical principles on an objective basis. I know of no other way of getting the teacher of composition out of the rut worn deep by generations treading the same round. One unrecognized virtue of counting in the study of style is that it compels a close look at the object, and one may be just lucky enough to hit upon something worth counting.

The most lucky find, the most radical insight to emerge from this inductive study, prompts the suggestion that our faith in the subordinate clause and the complex sentence is misplaced, that we should concentrate instead on the sentence modifiers, or free modifiers. It should suffice to point out that our school grammars and rhetorics would call the sentence by Hemingway on p. 8 a simple sentence, that in their view the third second-level element in the sentence by Clark on p. 10 is somehow more mature than the other three because it has a subordinate clause. But I will try to make the point another way. I have just read Ralph Ellison's *Invisible Man*, a great book, as remarkable for its style as for its insight into the mind of the "invisible man." I know of no textbook whose treatment of grammar and syntax could cope with more than a small fraction of its sentences, but I would venture the claim that there is not a sentence whose syntactic secrets could not be opened by the key fashioned in the first two essays.

Another point I want to emphasize is that the rhetorical analysis rests squarely on grammar. It should surprise no one that no experiments, or so it has been reported, show any correlation between knowledge of grammar and ability to write. One should not expect a correlation where no relation has been established and made the ground of the instruction. Many teachers, who don't want to teach composition anyway, use this as the negative of their argument that the only way to learn to write is to read literature. But what may be true over a lifetime is not true of the fifteen weeks of a semester. In practice, this position throws the burden of learning to write on the student. It expects him to divine the elements of style that make literature what it is and apply the relevant ones to writing expository essays about literature—a divination of which the teachers themselves are incapable. If reading literature were the royal road that this argument takes it to be, English teachers would be our best writers and *PMLA* would year by year take all the prizes for nonfiction.

A preface is the place to remember those who have helped to bring a book into being. I remember with special affection the many students in many classes, from freshmen to juniors and seniors with a sprinkling of graduates among them, who submitted cheerfully— with only one vocal exception—to a strange discipline. I remember the many teachers, my former students and others, who have tried out my ideas and reported on their practicability. The many program chairmen and directors of institutes and workshops who have invited me to talk. James Squire, Albert Kitzhaber and Robert Pooley, who first discerned "a something in the sky" and by their encouragement helped it take at last "a certain shape." The editors of the journals who accepted and printed these essays. Paul Olson and Frank Rice, directors of the Nebraska Curriculum Development Center, who made it possible for me to translate what I had written for teachers into a unit of their curriculum.[2]

Finally, I remember with special affection Elizabeth Hentley, who not only typed and retyped and proofread hundreds of pages but helped me see these pages as others would see them and saved me from many a blunder and perhaps some foolish notions.

F. C.

[2]The material written for the Nebraska Center is available as *The Rhetoric of Short Units of Composition* from the English Institute Materials Center, 4 Washington Place, New York, N.Y. 10003. With the permission of Paul Olson and the assistance of U. Harold Males, these materials are being put on transparencies for use with an overhead projector and together with a work book for students and a manual for teachers will be distributed by Harper & Row. The essays were written as prologue to a textbook, which, fate relenting, may appear before long.

A Generative Rhetoric of the Sentence

We do not have time in our classes to teach everything about the rhetoric of the sentence. I believe in "island hopping," concentrating on topics where we can produce results and leaving the rest, including the "comma splice" and the "run-on sentence," to die on the vine. The balanced sentence deserves some attention in discursive writing, and the enormous range of coordinate structures deserves a bit more. The rhythm of good

1

modern prose comes about equally from the multiple-tracking of coordinate constructions and the downshifting and backtracking of free modifiers. But the first comes naturally; the other needs coaxing along.

This coaxing is the clue to the meaning of *generative* in my title. (It is not derived from generative grammar; I used it before I ever heard of Chomsky.) The teacher can use the idea of levels of structure to urge the student to add further levels to what he has already produced, so that the structure itself becomes an aid to discovery.

This system of analysis by levels is essentially an application of immediate constituent analysis. IC analysis reveals what goes with what. In such analysis the free modifiers are cut off first. The order in which initial, medial, and final elements are cut off is immaterial, but one might as well start at the beginning. Thus, in sentence 2, the first cut would take off the whole set of initial modifiers. Then the members of a coordinate set are separated and, if the dissection is to be carried out to the ultimate constituents, analyzed one by one in order. In sentence 1, the first cut would come at the end of the base clause, taking off levels 2, 3, and 4 together since they are dependent on one another. Another cut would come at the end of level 2, taking off levels 3 and 4 together since 4 is a modifier of 3. Medial modifiers have to be cut *out* rather than *off*.

❧❧❧❧❧

If the new grammar is to be brought to bear on composition, it must be brought to bear on the rhetoric of the sentence. We have a workable and teachable, if not a definitive, modern grammar; but we do not have, despite several titles, a modern rhetoric.

In composition courses we do not really teach our captive charges to write better—we merely *expect* them to. And we do not teach them how to write better because we do not know how to teach them to write better. And so we merely go through the motions. Our courses with their tear-out work books and four-pound anthologies are elaborate evasions of the real problem. They permit us to put in our time and do almost anything else we'd rather be doing instead of buckling down to the hard work of making a difference in the student's understanding and manipulation of language.

With hundreds of handbooks and rhetorics to draw from, I have never been able to work out a program for teaching the sentence as I find it in the work of contemporary writers. The chapters on the sentence all adduce the traditional rhetorical classification of sentences as loose, balanced, and periodic. But the term *loose* seems to be taken as a pejorative (it sounds immoral); our students, no Bacons or Johnsons, have little occasion for balanced sentences; and some of our worst perversions of style come from the attempt to teach them to write periodic sentences. The traditional grammatical classification of sentences is equally barren. Its use in teaching composition rests on a semantic confusion, equating complexity of structure with complexity of thought and vice versa. But very simple thoughts may call for very complex grammatical constructions. Any moron can say "I don't know who done it." And some of us might be puzzled to work out the grammar of "All I want is all there is," although any chit can think it and say it and act on it.

The chapters on the sentence all appear to assume that we think naturally in primer sentences, progress naturally to compound sentences, and must be taught to combine the primer sentences into complex sentences— and that complex sentences are the mark of maturity. We need a rhetoric of the sentence that will do more than combine the ideas of primer sentences. We need one that will *generate* ideas.

For the foundation of such a generative or productive rhetoric I take the statement from John Erskine, the originator of the Great Books courses, himself a novelist. In an essay "The Craft of Writing" (*Twentieth Century English,* Philosophical Library, 1946) he discusses a principle of the writer's craft which, though known he says to all practitioners, he has never seen discussed in print. The principle is this: "When you write, you make a point, not by subtracting as though you sharpened a pencil, but by adding." We have all been told that the formula for good writing is the concrete noun and the active verb. Yet Erskine says, "What you say is found not in the noun but in what you add to qualify the noun . . . The noun, the verb, and the main clause serve merely as the base on which meaning will rise . . . The modifier is the essential part of any sentence." The foundation, then, for a generative or productive rhetoric of the sentence is that composition is essentially a process of *addition*.

But speech is linear, moving in time, and writing moves in linear space, which is analogous to time. When you add a modifier, whether to the noun, the verb, or the main clause, you must add it either before the head or after it. If you add it before the head, the direction of modification can be indicated by an arrow pointing forward; if you add it after, by an arrow pointing backward. Thus we have the second principle of a generative rhetoric—the principle of *direction of modification* or *direction of movement*.

Within the clause there is not much scope for operating with this principle. The positions of the various sorts of close, or restrictive, modifiers are generally fixed and the modifiers are often obligatory—"The man who came to dinner remained till midnight." Often the only choice is whether to add modifiers. What I have seen of attempts to bring structural grammar to bear on composition usually boils down to the injunction to "load the patterns." Thus "pattern practice" sets students to accreting sentences like this: "The small boy on the red bicycle who lives with his happy parents on our shady street often coasts down the steep street until he comes to the city park." This will never do. It has no rhythm and hence no life; it is tone-deaf. It is the seed that will burgeon into gobbledegook. One of the hardest things in writing is to keep the noun clusters and verb clusters short.

It is with modifiers added to the clause—that is, with sentence modifiers—that the principle comes into full play. The typical sentence of modern English, the kind we can best spend our efforts trying to teach, is what we may call the *cumulative sentence*. The main clause, which may or may not have a sentence modifier before it, advances the discussion; but the additions move backward, as in this clause, to modify the statement of the main clause or more often to explicate or exemplify it, so that the sentence has a flowing and ebbing movement, advancing to a new position and then pausing to consolidate it, leaping and lingering as the popular ballad does. The first part of the preceding compound sentence has one addition, placed within it; the second part has 4 words in the main clause and 49 in the five additions placed after it.

The cumulative sentence is the opposite of the periodic sentence. It does not represent the idea as conceived, pondered over, reshaped, packaged, and delivered cold. It is dynamic rather than static, representing the mind thinking. The main clause ("the additions move backward" above) exhausts the mere fact of the idea; logically, there is nothing more to say. The additions stay with the same idea, probing its bearings and implications, exemplifying it or seeking an analogy or metaphor for it, or reducing it to details. Thus the mere form of the sentence generates ideas. It serves the needs of both the writer and the reader, the writer by compelling him to examine his thought, the reader by letting him into the writer's thought.

Addition and direction of movement are structural principles. They involve the grammatical character of the sentence. Before going on to other principles, I must say a word about the best grammar as the foundation for rhetoric. I cannot conceive any useful transactions between teacher and students unless they have in common a language for talking about sentences. The best grammar for the present purpose is the grammar that best displays the layers of structure of the English sentence. The best I have found in a textbook is the combination of immediate constituent and transformation grammar in Paul Roberts's *English Sentences*. Traditional grammar, whether over-simple as in the school tradition or over-complex as in the scholarly tradition, does not reveal the language as it operates; it leaves everything, to borrow a phrase from Wordsworth, "in disconnection dead and spiritless." *English Sentences* is oversimplified and it has gaps, but it displays admirably the structures that rhetoric must work with—primarily sentence modifiers, including nonrestrictive relative and subordinate clauses, but, far more important, the array of noun, verb, and adjective clusters. It is paradoxical that Professor Roberts, who has done so much to make the teaching of composition possible, should himself be one of those who think that it cannot be taught. Unlike Ulysses, he does not see any work for Telemachus to work.

Layers of structure, as I have said, is a grammatical concept. To bring in the dimension of meaning, we need a third principle—that of *levels of generality* or *levels of abstraction*. The main or base clause is likely to be stated in general or abstract or plural terms. With the main clause stated, the forward movement of the sentence stops, the writer shifts down to a lower level of generality or abstraction or to singular terms, and goes back over the same ground at this lower level.[1] There is no theoretical limit to the number of structural layers or levels, each[2] at a lower level of generality, any or all of them compounded, that a speaker or writer may use. For a speaker, listen to Lowell Thomas; for a writer, study Wil-

---

[1] Cf. Leo Rockas "Abstract and Concrete Sentences," *CCC*, May 1963. Rockas describes sentences as abstract or concrete, the abstract implying the concrete and vice versa. Readers and writers, he says, must have the knack of apprehending the concrete in the abstract and the abstract in the concrete. This is true and valuable. I am saying that within a single sentence the writer may present more than one level of generality, translating the abstract into the more concrete in added levels.

[2] This statement is not quite tenable. Each helps to make the idea of the base clause more concrete or specific, but each is not more concrete or specific than the one immediately above it. See pp. 56, 80.

liam Faulkner. To a single independent clause he may
append a page of additions, but usually all clear, all
grammatical, once we have learned how to read him. Or,
if you prefer, study Hemingway, the master of the simple sentence: "George was coming down in the telemark
position, kneeling, one leg forward and bent, the other
trailing, his sticks hanging like some insect's thin legs,
kicking up puffs of snow, and finally the whole kneeling,
trailing figure coming around in a beautiful right curve,
crouching, the legs shot forward and back, the body
leaning out against the swing, the sticks accenting the
curve like points of light, all in a wild cloud of snow."
Only from the standpoint of school grammar is this a
simple sentence.

This brings me to the fourth, and last, principle, that
of texture. *Texture* provides a descriptive or evaluative
term. If a writer adds to few of his nouns or verbs or
main clauses and adds little, the texture may be said to
be thin. The style will be plain or bare. The writing of
most of our students is thin—even threadbare. But if he
adds frequently or much or both, then the texture may
be said to be dense or rich. One of the marks of an effective style, especially in narrative, is variety in the texture,
the texture varying with the change in pace, the varia-
tion in texture producing the change in pace. It is not
true, as I have seen it asserted, that fast action calls for
short sentences; the action is fast in the sentence by
Hemingway above. In our classes, we have to work for
greater density and variety in texture and greater con-
creteness and particularity in what is added.

I have been operating at a fairly high level of generality. Now I must downshift and go over the same

points with examples. The most graphic way to exhibit the layers of structure is to indent the word groups of a sentence and to number the levels. The first three sentences illustrate the various positions of the added sentence modifiers—initial, medial, and final. The symbols mark the grammatical character of the additions: SC, subordinate clause; RC, relative clause; NC, noun cluster; VC, verb cluster; AC, adjective cluster; A + A, adjective series; Abs, absolute (i.e., a VC with a subject of its own); PP, prepositional phrase. The elements set off as on a lower level are marked as sentence modifiers by junctures or punctuation. The examples have been chosen to illustrate the range of constructions used in the lower levels; after the first few they are arranged by the number of levels. The examples could have been drawn from poetry as well as from prose. Those not attributed are by students.

1

1 He dipped his hands in the bichloride solution and shook them,
  2 a quick shake, (NC)
    3 fingers down, (Abs)
      4 like the fingers of a pianist above the keys. (PP)

Sinclair Lewis

2

  2 Calico-coated, (AC)
  2 small-bodied, (AC)
    3 with delicate legs and pink faces in which their mismatched eyes rolled wild and subdued, (PP)
1 they huddled,
  2 gaudy motionless and alert, (A + A)
  2 wild as deer, (AC)
  2 deadly as rattlesnakes, (AC)
  2 quiet as doves. (AC)

William Faulkner

3

1 The bird's eye, / , remained fixed upon him;
   2 / bright and silly as a sequin (AC)
1 its little bones, / , seemed swooning in his hand.
   2 / wrapped . . . in a warm padding of feathers (VC)

Stella Benson

4

1 The jockeys sat bowed and relaxed,
   2 moving a little at the waist with the movement of their
     horses. (VC)

Katherine Anne Porter

5

1 The flame sidled up the match,
   2 driving a film of moisture and a thin strip of darker grey
     before it. (VC)

6

1 She came among them behind the man,
   2 gaunt in the gray shapeless garment and the sunbonnet,
     (AC)
   2 wearing stained canvas gymnasium shoes. (VC)

Faulkner

7

1 The Texan turned to the nearest gatepost and climbed to
   the top of it,
   2 his alternate thighs thick and bulging in the tight
     trousers, (Abs)
   2 the butt of the pistol catching and losing the sun in
     pearly gleams. (Abs)

Faulkner

8

1 He could sail for hours,
   2 searching the blanched grasses below him with his
     telescopic eyes, (VC)
   2 gaining height against the wind, (VC)
   2 descending in mile-long, gently declining swoops when
     he curved and rode back, (VC)
   2 never beating a wing. (VC)

Walter Van Tilburg Clark

9

1 They regarded me silently,
   2 Brother Jack with a smile that went no deeper than his lips, (Abs)
      3 his head cocked to one side, (Abs)
      3 studying me with his penetrating eyes; (VC)
   2 the other blank-faced, (Abs)
      3 looking out of eyes that were meant to reveal nothing and to stir profound uncertainty. (VC)

Ralph Ellison

10

1 He stood at the top of the stairs and watched me,
   2 I waiting for him to call me up, (Abs)
   2 he hesitating to come down, (Abs)
      3 his lips nervous with the suggestion of a smile, (Abs)
      3 mine asking whether the smile meant come, or go away. (Abs)

11

1 Joad's lips stretched tight over his long teeth for a moment, and
1 he licked his lips,
   2 like a dog, (PP)
      3 two licks, (NC)
         4 one in each direction from the middle. (NC)

Steinbeck

12

1 We all live in two realities:
   2 one of seeming fixity, (NC)
      3 with institutions, dogmas, rules of punctuation, and routines, (PP)
         4 the calendared and clockwise world of all but futile round on round; (NC) and
   2 one of whirling and flying electrons, dreams, and possibilities, (NC)
      3 behind the clock. (PP)

Sidney Cox

13

1 It was as though someone, somewhere, had touched a lever and shifted gears, and

1 the hospital was set for night running,
  2 smooth and silent, (A + A)
  2 its normal clatter and hum muffled, (Abs)
  2 the only sounds heard in the whitewalled room distant and unreal: (Abs)
    3 a low hum of voices from the nurses' desk, (NC)
      4 quickly stifled, (VC)
    3 the soft squish of rubber-soled shoes on the tiled corridor, (NC)
    3 starched white cloth rustling against itself, (NC) and, outside,
    3 the lonesome whine of wind in the country night (NC) and
    3 the Kansas dust beating against the windows. (NC)
14
1 The beach sounds are jazzy,
  2 percussion fixing the mode—(Abs)
    3 the surf cracking and booming in the distance, (Abs)
    3 a little nearer dropped bar-bells clanking, (Abs)
    3 steel gym rings, / , ringing, (Abs)
    /4 flung together, (VC)
    3 palm fronds rustling above me, (Abs)
      4 like steel brushes washing over a snare drum, (PP)
    3 troupes of sandals splatting and shuffling on the sandy cement, (Abs)
      4 their beat varying, (Abs)
        5 syncopation emerging and disappearing with changing paces. (Abs)
15
1 A small Negro girl develops from the sheet of glare-frosted walk,
  2 walking barefooted, (VC)
    3 her bare legs striking and coiling from the hot cement, (Abs)
      4 her feet curling in, (Abs)
        5 only the outer edges touching. (Abs)
16
1 The swells moved rhythmically toward us,
  2 irregularly faceted, (VC)

  2 sparkling, (VC)
  2 growing taller and more powerful until the shining crest
    bursts, (VC)
    3 a transparent sheet of pale green water spilling over
      the top, (Abs)
      4 breaking into blue-white foam as it cascades down
        the front of the wave, (VC)
      4 piling up in a frothy mound that the diminishing
        wave pushes up against the pilings, (VC)
        5 with a swishsmash, (PP)
      4 the foam drifting back, (Abs)
        5 like a lace fan opened over the shimmering water
          as the spent wave returns whispering to the
          sea. (PP)

The best starting point for a composition unit based
on these four principles is with two-level narrative sentences, first with one second-level addition (sentences 4,
5), then with two or more parallel ones (6, 7, 8). Anyone
sitting in his room with his eyes closed could write the
main clause of most of the examples; the discipline comes
with the additions, provided they are based at first on
immediate observation, requiring the student to phrase
an exact observation in exact language. This can hardly
fail to be exciting to a class: it is life, with the variety
and complexity of life; the workbook exercise is death.
The situation is ideal also for teaching diction—abstract-
concrete, general-specific, literal-metaphorical, denota-
tive-connotative. When the sentences begin to come out
right, it is time to examine the additions for their grammatical character. From then on the grammar comes to
the aid of the writing and the writing reinforces the
grammar. One can soon go on to multi-level narrative
sentences (1, 9–11, 15, 16) and then to brief narratives of
three to six or seven sentences on actions with a begin-

ning, a middle, and an end that can be observed over and over again—beating eggs, making a cut with a power saw, or following a record changer's cycle or a wave's flow and ebb. (Bring the record changer to class.) Description, by contrast, is static, picturing appearance rather than behavior. The constructions to master are the noun and adjective clusters and the absolute (13, 14). Then the descriptive noun cluster must be taught to ride piggy-back on the narrative sentence, so that description and narration are interleaved: "In the morning we went out into a new world, a glistening crystal and white world, each skeleton tree, each leafless bush, even the heavy, drooping power lines sheathed in icy crystal." The next step is to develop the sense for variety in texture and change in pace that all good narrative demands.

In the next unit, the same four principles can be applied to the expository paragraph. But this is a subject for another paper.

I want to anticipate two possible objections. One is that the sentences are long. By freshman English standards they are long, but I could have produced far longer ones from works freshmen are expected to read. Of the sentences by students, most were written as finger exercises in the first few weeks of the course. I try in narrative sentences to push to level after level, not just two or three, but four, five, or six, even more, as far as the students' powers of observation will take them. I want them to become sentence acrobats, to dazzle by their syntactic dexterity. I'd rather have to deal with hyperemia than anemia. I want to add my voice to that of James Coleman (*CCC*, December 1962) deploring our concentration on the plain style.

The other objection is that my examples are mainly

descriptive and narrative—and today in freshman English we teach only exposition. I deplore this limitation as much as I deplore our limitation to the plain style. Both are a sign that we have sold our proper heritage for a pot of message. In permitting them, the English department undercuts its own discipline. Even if our goal is only utilitarian prose, we can teach diction and sentence structure far more effectively through a few controlled exercises in description and narration than we can by starting right off with exposition (Theme One, 500 words, precipitates *all* the problems of writing). There is no problem of invention; the student has something to communicate—his immediate sense impressions, which can stand a bit of exercising. The material is not already verbalized—he has to match language to sense impressions. His acuteness in observation and in choice of words can be judged by fairly objective standards—is the sound of a bottle of milk being set down on a concrete step suggested better by *clink* or *clank* or *clunk?* In the examples, study the diction for its accuracy, rising at times to the truly imaginative. Study the use of metaphor, of comparison. This verbal virtuosity and syntactical ingenuity can be made to carry over into expository writing.

But this is still utilitarian. What I am proposing carries over of itself into the study of literature. It makes the student a better reader of literature. It helps him thread the syntactical mazes of much mature writing, and it gives him insight into that elusive thing we call style. Last year a student told of rereading a book by her favorite author, Willa Cather, and of realizing for the first time *why* she liked reading her: she could understand and appreciate the style. For some students, moreover, such writing makes life more interesting as well as giving them a way to share their interest with others. When they learn how to put concrete details into a sentence, they begin to look at life with more alertness. If it is liberal education we are concerned with, it is just possible that these things are more important than anything we can achieve when we set our sights on the plain style in expository prose.

I want to conclude with a historical note. My thesis in this paragraph is that modern prose like modern poetry has more in common with the seventeenth than with the eighteenth century and that we fail largely because we are operating from an eighteenth century base. The shift from the complex to the cumulative sentence is more profound than it seems. It goes deep in grammar, requiring a shift from the subordinate clause (the staple of our trade) to the cluster and the absolute (so little understood as to go almost unnoticed in our textbooks). And I have only lately come to see that this shift has historical implications. The cumulative sentence is the modern form of the loose sentence that characterized the anti-Ciceronian movement in the seventeenth century. This movement, according to Morris W. Croll[3], began with Montaigne and Bacon and continued with such men as Donne, Browne, Taylor, Pascal. To Montaigne, its art was the art of being natural; to Pascal, its eloquence was the eloquence that mocks formal eloquence; to Bacon, it presented knowledge so that it could be examined, not so that it must be accepted.

---

[3]"The Baroque Style in Prose," *Studies in English Philology: A Miscellany in Honor of Frederick Klaeber* (1929), reprinted in *Style, Rhetoric, and Rhythm: Essays by Morris W. Croll* (1966) and A. M. Witherspoon and F. J. Warnke, *Seventeenth-Century Prose and Poetry*, 2nd ed. (1963). I have borrowed from Croll in my description of the cumulative sentence.

But the Senecan amble was banished from England when "the direct sensuous apprehension of thought" (T. S. Eliot's words) gave way to Cartesian reason or intellect. The consequences of this shift in sensibility are well summarized by Croll:

> To this mode of thought we are to trace almost all the features of modern literary education and criticism, or at least of what we should have called modern a generation ago: the study of the precise meaning of words; the reference to dictionaries as literary authorities; the study of the sentence as a logical unit alone; the careful circumscription of its limits and the gradual reduction of its length; . . .[4] the attempt to reduce grammar to an exact science; the idea that forms of speech are always either correct or incorrect; the complete subjection of the laws of motion and expression in style to the laws of logic and standardization —in short, the triumph, during two centuries, of grammatical over rhetorical ideas.

Here is a seven-point scale any teacher of composition can use to take stock. He can find whether he is based in the eighteenth century or in the twentieth and whether he is consistent—completely either an ancient or a modern—or is just a crazy mixed-up kid.

❦❦❦❦❦

POSTSCRIPT

I have asserted that "syntactical ingenuity" can best be developed in narrative-descriptive writing and that

---

[4]The omitted item concerns punctuation and is not relevant here. In using this scale, note the phrase "what we should have called modern a generation ago" and remember that Croll was writing in 1929.

it can be made to carry over into discursive writing. The count made for the article on sentence openers included all sentence modifiers—or free modifiers, as I prefer to call them. In the total number of free modifiers, the 2000 word samples were almost identical—1545 in the fiction and 1519 in the nonfiction, roughly one in three sentences out of four. But they differ in position:

Nonfiction	initial 575	medial 492	final 452
Fiction	initial 404	medial 329	final 812

And they differ in some of the grammatical kinds used in the final position:

Nonfiction	NC 123	VC 63	Abs 9
Fiction	NC 131	VC 218	Abs 108

Thus the differences are not in the structures used, only in the position and in the frequency of the various kinds of structures. It will be well to look at a few more sentences of discursive prose.

17

1 His [Hemingway's] characters, / , wander through the ruins of Babel,
  2/ expatriates for the most part, (NC)
  2 smattering many tongues (VC) and
  2 speaking a demotic version of their own. (VC)

Harry Levin

18

1 From literal to figurative is one range that a word may take:
  2 from *foot* of a person to *foot* of a mountain, (PP)
    3 a substituted or metaphoric use. (NC)

1 From concrete to abstract is another range:
  2 from *foot* to *extremity*, (PP)

3 stressing one of the abstract characteristics of foot, (VC)
    4 a contrast for which the terms *image* and *symbol* as distinguished from *concept* are also used. (NC)

Josephine Miles

19

2 Going back to his [Hemingway's] work in 1944, (VC)
1 you perceive his kinship with a wholly different group of novelists,
    2 let us say with Poe and Hawthorne and Melville: (PP)
        3 the haunted and nocturnal writers, (NC)
        3 the men who dealt in images that were symbols of an inner world. (NC)

Malcolm Cowley

20

1 Even her style in it is transitional and momentous,
    2 a matter of echoing and reminiscing effects, and of little clarion notes of surprise and prophecy here and there; (NC)
        3 befitting that time of life which has been called the old age of youth and the youth of old age, (AC or VC)
            4 a time fraught with heartache and youthful tension. (NC)

Glenway Wescott, of Colette's *Break of Day*

21

2 Aglow with splendor and consequence, (AC)
1 he [Sterne] rejoined his wife and daughter,
    2 whom he presently transferred to his new parsonage at Coxwold, (RC)
        3 an old and rambling house, (NC)
            4 full of irregular, comfortable rooms, (AC)
            4 situated on the edge of the moors, (VC)
                5 in a neighborhood much healthier than the marshy lands of Sutton. (PP)

Peter Quennell

22

1 It is with the coming of man that a vast hole seems to open
   in nature,
  2 a vast black whirlpool spinning faster and faster, (NC)
    3 consuming flesh, stones, soil, minerals, (VC)
    3 sucking down the lightning, (VC)
    3 wrenching power from the atom, (VC)
      4 until the ancient sounds of nature are drowned out
        in the cacophony of something which is no longer
        nature, (SC)
        5 something instead which is loose and knocking at
          the world's heart, (NC)
        5 something demonic and no longer planned—(NC)
          6 escaped, it may be—(VC)
          6 spewed out of nature, (VC)
          6 contending in a final giant's game against its
            master. (VC)

                                  Loren Eiseley

The structures used in prose are necessarily the structures used in poetry, necessarily because prose and
poetry use the same language. Poets may take more
liberties with the grammar than prose writers are likely
to do; but their departures from the norm must all be
understood by reference to the norm. Since poets, like
the writers of narrative, work more by association than
by logical connection, their sentences are likely to have
similar structures. They seem to know the values of the
cumulative sentence.

The first example here consists of the first two stanzas
of "The Meadow Mouse"; the slashes mark the line ends.
The other example constitutes the last four of the five
stanzas of "The Motive for Metaphor." It shows well
how structural analysis of the sentence reveals the tactics
of a difficult poem.

23

1 In a shoebox stuffed in an old nylon stocking / Sleeps the baby mouse I found in the meadow, /
  2 Where he trembled and shook beneath a stick / Till I caught him up by the tail and brought him in, / (RC)
    3 Cradled in my hand, / (VC)
    3 a little quaker, (NC)
      4 the whole body of him trembling, / (Abs)
    3 His absurd whiskers sticking out like a cartoon mouse, / (Abs)
    3 His feet like small leaves, / (Abs)
      4 Little lizard-feet, / (NC)
      4 Whitish and spread wide when he tried to struggle away, / (AC)
        5 Wriggling like a minuscule puppy. (VC)

1 Now he's eaten his three kinds of cheese and drunk from his bottle-cap watering trough— /
  2 So much he just lies in one corner, / (AC)
    3 His tail curled under him, (Abs)
    3 his belly big / As his head, (Abs)
    3 His bat-like ears / Twitching, (Abs)
      4 tilting toward the least sound. (VC)

                    Theodore Roethke

24

  2 In the same way, (PP)
1 you were happy in spring,
  2 with the half colors of quarter-things, (PP)
    3 The slightly brighter sky, (NC)
    3 the melting clouds, (NC)
    3 the single bird, (NC)
    3 the obscure moon—(NC)
      4 The obscure moon lighting an obscure world of things that would never be quite expressed, (NC)
        5 where you yourself were never quite yourself and did not want nor have to be, (RC)
          6 desiring the exhilarations of changes: (VC)
            7 the motive for metaphor, (NC)

6 shrinking from the weight of primary noon,
   (VC)
7 the ABC of being, (NC)
7 the ruddy temper, (NC)
7 the hammer of red and blue, (NC)
7 the hard sound—(NC)
   8 steel against intimation—(NC)
7 the sharp flash, (NC)
7 the vital, arrogant, fatal, dominant X. (NC)
                                    Wallace Stevens

❦❦❦❦❦❦❦❦❦❦❦❦❦❦❦❦

A Lesson from Hemingway

This essay was the first written of the four major ones reprinted in this volume. It is an outgrowth of my first realization that with the materials then available I could not teach students to write better but could only expect them to. Help came from an unlikely source—from Max Eastman's happy-thoughted book *Enjoyment of Poetry*. I wish that every teacher might read this book before reading my essay. In the sixth chapter, "Choice and

23

Comparison in Poetry," he would find three of my key terms—*quality, part* (or *detail*), and *comparison*. The idea of levels, with the stages of naming and adding, is implicit in the same chapter. I have used the essay by John Erskine as a convenient expository device, but the clues I have followed came in the first place from Eastman.

If I had written this essay in the sixties, some details would have been handled differently and some phrased differently, but there would have been no basic differences. The main difference would be a sharper distinction between modifiers that are set off and those that are not, between what I came to call later free and bound modifiers.

❦❦❦❦❦

Several years ago, in "A Note on the Writer's Craft" (*Twentieth Century English*, New York, 1946), John Erskine discussed a "principle" which he said is known to every writer but which he had never seen discussed in print. It illustrates, he says incidentally, "the startling gulf between the grammar which is taught and learned and the grammar which is used." The principle is this:

> When you write, you make a point, not by subtracting as though you sharpened a pencil, but by adding. When you put one word after another, your statement should be more precise the more you add. If the result is otherwise, you have added the wrong thing, or you have added more than was needed.
>   . . . the grammarian leaves with the unwary the impression that the substantive, since it can stand alone, is more

important than the adjective, that the verb is more important than the adverb, that the main clause is more important than the subordinate.

In the use of language, however, the truth is precisely the reverse. What you wish to say is found not in the noun but in what you add to qualify the noun. The noun is only a grappling iron to hitch your mind to the reader's. The noun by itself adds nothing to the reader's information; it is the name of something he knows already, and if he does not know it, you cannot do business with him. The noun, the verb, and the main clause serve merely as a base on which the meaning will rise.

The modifier is the essential part of any sentence.

Erskine did not develop this principle to any extent. I have attempted to do so for descriptive and narrative, or descriptive-narrative, writing, putting the problem this way: what does a writer add to the noun and the verb and the main clause to make a point—that is, to give to the image the degree and kind of particularity his purpose requires and his sensibility and experience permit?

My purpose in this has been practical rather than theoretical. The style is the man and style cannot be taught, the clichés run. But style is not a seamless robe, and one might by analysis, I thought, determine some of the elements of a concrete style—elements common to all individual styles in the way the elements of syntax are common—and apply such an analysis in teaching composition. Mr. Kempton has said (*The Short Story*, Cambridge, Mass., 1948) that it is "the attempt of fiction to refrain from full explanation but maintain intelligibility and interest by a thin but ceaseless stream of concrete details. . . . Something like a continuum of existence is what the storyteller is after." The ability to summon and manage that thin stream or continuum may be a gift

which cannot be communicated, though that is what
courses in fiction writing must occupy themselves with.
But the means of making the details concrete, or graphic
and telling, can be studied as a separate element of style.
The thin stream carries the nouns and verbs and main
clauses, so to speak, and what may be added to sharpen
the image can be made the subject of study and practice.

And not only that. "Nothing is clear until we have put
it into words," Bergson says, "for words are the only
means of translating impressions to the intellect. Hence
the immense help expression gives to vision, in clarifying
it. The growth of the power of language is not merely a
technical development, it implies a growth of vision." If
this is true, then learning to sharpen an image is learning
to see an image sharply. It is not so much that we only
see what we are looking for as that we are not likely to
see what we cannot see how to use. In short, growth in
the kind of vision that counts in writing requires a focus
and a medium.

Erskine's statement of his principle is put in grammatical terms, but the analysis can also be made in what
I will call rhetorical terms; and since the rhetorical terms,
illustrated from description rather than from narration,
afford the simplest starting point, we can begin with any
simple descriptive passage which exemplifies the various
possibilities, such as this from Peattie's *An Almanac for
Moderns* on learning to distinguish deciduous trees in
winter:

> Only gradually one finds he too is learning the subtlest
> differences where at first all seems alike: the BRANCHES OF
> IRONWOOD, *like the muscles of a straining wrestler,* the
> SHAPES OF ELMS *like a falling fountain,* the *mottled* BARK

OF SYCAMORES, the ALDERS *with their little cones,* the
HICKORIES *with their buds almost like flowers*—out of the
silvery winter ranks individuals step forth, are marked,
remembered.—January 25th.

The first statement, down to the colon, motivates the
addition of description. The nouns in small capitals name
the items the author has chosen to present; they are the
headwords to which description is added. The italicized
parts are what has been added to sharpen the image—to
distinguish individuals where at first all was alike.

The simplest way to individualize a thing is to point
to some *quality* or *attribute,* as "mottled" does. The
second way is to point to some *part* of the object, what I
will call a *detail.* Here the alders are marked by their
cones, the hickories by their buds. Pointing to a quality
effects in the reader's mind an over-all modification of
the image suggested by the headword; it is like turning
the focusing knob and seeing the blurred image spring
into sharpness on the ground glass. Pointing to a detail,
on the other hand, is like moving in for a close-up of
some part of the tree. The third way is to go beyond the
object itself and to sharpen the image by suggesting its
likeness to something else, as is done here with the
branches of ironwood and the shapes of elms. Consider-
able experience has convinced me that there are only
these three *methods of description,* as I will call them—
by qualities or attributes, by details, and by comparison.
Adjectives such as *exhilarating* suggest a fourth, by
effect, but this soon shades off into explanation. It should
be noted that the nouns in what is added may in turn
become headwords and have description of their own—
straining, falling, little, almost like flowers. Any of the

three methods may be used for such further-level description, and there is no limit to the number of levels. The description here is all drawn from the sense of sight, but it may be drawn from any of the senses.

From the point of view of grammar the matter is a little more complicated. A quality or attribute is always designated by an adjective, but an adjective does not always designate a quality. It may designate a detail, *thin-barked*, or a comparison, *flower-like* or *flower-soft;* and an abstract adjective, such as *beautiful*, does not picture at all but summarizes, and should be regarded as expository. The detail usually calls for a phrase—a prepositional phrase (most commonly *with, without,* or *in*) or a participial or absolute phrase. The comparison usually calls for a *like*-phrase. Any of the three may be given the weight of a predicate—"The bark of the sycamore is mottled"; "Hickories have buds, and the buds are almost like flowers." But a separate predication interrupts the narrative movement and tends toward exposition.

This, then, is what a writer may add to a noun to sharpen the picture of an *object*. He does exactly the same thing when the headword is a verb and he wants to sharpen the picture of an *action*. He uses the same three methods of description. (A separate term, *methods of narration*, seems hardly necessary.) He points to some quality or detail of the action or he suggests a comparison. (We are concerned here only with adverbs of manner or attendant circumstances; adverbs of time, place, etc., take care of themselves.) Even the grammatical character of the additions is identical, except that adverbs usually take the place of adjectives.

For the rest of this paper I have chosen to narrow the

discussion from what *may* be added to what one author actually *did* add, hoping thus to give some notion of the frequency of the various kinds of modifiers. I have narrowed it still further to what has been added to the *verb,* in other words, to narration. The piece chosen, Hemingway's *The Undefeated,* has the advantage of a relatively simple narrative style and of being close to pure narrative, with almost no intermixture of description or explanation. It will pass too, I suppose, for expert narration; Edward J. O'Brien, who includes it in his *Short Story Case Book,* says, "Ernest Hemingway's duel with words is as close and skilful a struggle as Manuel's with the bull."

In applying Erskine's principle to this story, I have confined my counting to the scenes at the bullring, though I have taken examples from the opening and closing scenes at the office, cafe, and infirmary. Dialog and interior monolog are excluded as belonging to the characters rather than to the author. My count shows that in the bullring scenes Hemingway used 668 predicate verbs, plus 17 sentences without predicate verbs, to sustain the stream of narrative action. Of these, 532 stand alone without modifiers of the kind we are concerned with, and 153, or one in every four or five, have modifiers. The total number of modifiers added is 236, some of which, of course, are second-level modifiers. A frequency such as this, especially when the modifiers are mainly of the relatively long types, results in a style that may be said to have a relatively dense *texture.* By comparison, the opening and closing scenes, with fewer and lighter modifiers, have a lighter texture. This concept of texture as determined by the frequency and the rhetorical and grammatical character of the modifiers and whether they are used for description or narration is useful for understanding and comparing individual styles.

In the bullring scenes Hemingway uses comparison 7 times, description by quality 35 times, and details 194 times. The proportions are 1:5:28. In almost any prose, I believe, the three methods will stand in this order, but the proportions will vary enormously.

His sparing use of comparison is what one might expect in writing where there is no play of fancy over the surface of the material. The few comparisons he does use, though, are models for a style that chooses for its immediate effect a camera-like precision in following the action. They are all simple, familiar, and appropriate to the action. The bullfighter's cape "swung out like a ballet dancer's skirt" and he "wound the bull around himself like a belt"; he pricked the cape with the tip of his sword and with the sword "spread the red flannel like the jib of a boat"; knocked to the ground and lying on his back, he fended off the bull by "kicking like a man keeping a ball in the air"; "At the end of the pass the bull turned like a cat coming around a corner and faced Manuel."

Hemingway is not given much, either, to describing an action by its quality or attributes, that is, by the use of adverbs; there are only 17 of them, or 1 to 48 verbs. This is to be expected in a writer who cares for exact rather than general effects, because the adverb of manner is no tool for a precise workman. Most of such adverbs are abstract, and the common concrete ones are mostly general rather than specific. When a writer experiments with the adverb, as Robert Penn Warren and Truman Capote have done, the adverb usually calls attention to itself: "He heard the ice settle *clinkingly* in the full glass" (Warren); "A firefly pulsing *goldenly*" (Capote). In *The Undefeated* the adverbs concerned with the horses and bulls are faintly concrete; the best one suggests rather well the quality of the horses provided by Retana: "The picadors galloped *jerkily* around the ring." But the abstract adverbs defining the attitude of Hernandez and Fuentes are an indulgent shortcut: said *cheerfully* or *happily*, walking *arrogantly* or *insultingly*.

In this story more adjectives than adverbs (18 as against 17) are added to the verb, and they are more interesting. Seven of them are complements rather than modifiers—that is, predicate adjectives used after verbs of action rather than after "empty" copulas. These "quasi-predicatives," as Jespersen calls them, make it possible to combine description with narration, so that the reader can picture the agent in the course or at the end of the action: as the sword was withdrawn, "the scabbard fell *limp*"; the gypsy was "watching *lazy-eyed*"; the sword "shot up in the air . . . to fall *red-hilted* on the sand." Others differ from these in standing outside the clause, in the appositive position. The examples in this story are not remarkable: "The bull stood, *heavy* and *dull* again after the action"; "There was the bull standing, *heavy*, firmly planted"; " 'You ever seen these fellows?' Zurito asked, *big* and *looming* beside Manuel in the dark." Although Hemingway has not used them freely, such appositive adjectives are a characteristic feature of the loosely cumulative sentences of modern descriptive-narrative style. Finally, an adjective sometimes turns up in a series of adverbial modifiers, so that description and narration are interwoven: "There he came, eyes open, *ugly*, watching the cape"; "Fuentes stood watching, his cape held against his body, *tall,* in repose, watching lazy-eyed."

The most important, by far, of the methods of describing action is by details; in this story there are 5 for every adjective and adverb and 28 for every comparison. And they are important not only in numbers but in what a writer can do with them.

I have defined a detail as a part of any given whole. In narration the "whole" is the unit of action, the segment of the continuum, named by the headword. Take, for example, this sentence from the cafe scene: "In the far corner the man WAS still ASLEEP, *snoring slightly on the intaking breath, his head back against the wall.*" The "whole" is the situation blocked out by the predicate of the main clause, WAS ASLEEP; the italicized phrases are the "parts," the details of the action of sleeping. A few more examples will make clear this principle: He READ the newspaper laboriously, *forming the words with his lips as he read*"; "He felt the sword buckle[1]. . . and then it SHOT high in the air, *end-over-ending into the crowd.*" In each sentence, the italicized phrase sharpens the image by designating an action, or sometimes an attitude or posture ("his head back against the wall"), that is a subordinate part of that proposed by the headword. Though the term *detail* is convenient and will be used here, *attendant circumstances* would sometimes be more accurate: "He sat heavily in his chair, *his black cordoba hat tipped forward.*"

Descriptive details can be compressed to an adjective and are occasionally expanded to a relative clause; but narrative details are practically restricted to phrases as

---

[1]*Buckle* here is an infinitive, not a noun.

their vehicle. The phrases are again of three kinds—prepositional, participial, absolute.

The prepositional phrase, with the same prepositions (*with, without,* and *in*), is far less common in narration than in description. In narration the preposition is a device for converting nouns to an adverbial function, and the use of the phrase is limited by the vocabulary available. Most of the nouns could be used directly as verbs, but there is a difference in emphasis between "The bull *rushed* out" and "The bull came out *in a rush.*" Moreover, the modifiers to be used sometimes determine the choice of noun or verb. In sentences such as these— ". . . with prissy little sidling steps, she started forward" and "He advanced along the shore with a creeping bowlegged hobble" (Capote)—*step* and *hobble* could not be used as verbs because their modifiers could not be converted to adverbs.

Of the 13 prepositional phrases in *The Undefeated,* 9 are based on *in* and only 4 on *with,* an unusual proportion. The *in*-phrases are all simple: "Then the bull came out *in a rush,* skidding on his four legs as he came out under the lights, then charging *in a gallop,* moving softly *in a fast gallop*"; "The bull charged *in a scramble*"; "The gypsy moved *in a zigzag.*" None of Hemingway's are typical *with*-phrases like the two from Capote quoted above. They should, strictly, be classed as absolute phrases. In a sentence such as this—"The bull, *with his tongue out, his barrel heaving,* was watching the gypsy" —the two phrases are identical except for *with,* and *with* here is simply a "marker" of the absolute.

Participial and absolute phrases are more useful vehicles for narrative details because they use a form of the verb instead of a noun. The two differ in that the subject of the participle is not contained in the phrase itself but must be inferred from other parts of the sentence, whereas the absolute has its own subject. The absolute is the ideal vehicle for details, descriptive as well as narrative, because any part of the agent or the situation can be singled out for separate notice. This can be seen in a sentence where both kinds of phrases are used in a series: "Manuel SWUNG with the charge, *sweeping the muleta ahead of the bull, his feet firm, the sword following the curve,* a point of light under the arcs." *Manuel,* the subject of *swung,* is also the subject in a secondary way of *sweeping;* but Hemingway wants us to see, as parts of the same action, the feet held firm, the sword, in the other hand, following the curve of the muleta. If it were not for the absolute construction he would have to say something like "sweeping the muleta ahead of the bull, holding his feet firm, following the curve with his sword," which would not only be clumsy and wordy but put the three subordinate actions on the same plane. Finally, as a detail within a detail, he wants us to see the sword as not a sword but a point of light. The construction is a noun cluster or phrase.

The participle, the lighter of these two constructions, appears more frequently; there are two for each absolute phrase. The 121 include 11 passive participles and 11 "fused" participles, that is, participles that are not separated by punctuation from the verb they modify: "The little man sat looking at him" as contrasted with "Retana sat, saying nothing and looking at Manuel." There are 60 absolute phrases, not counting the 17 punctuated as sentences.

How Hemingway has handled details can be shown

best by examples where he seems most intent on shaping the sentence to the action, trying to get the complexity of the action without losing the narrative continuity. This will show, too, all three methods working together and all the grammatical forms they express themselves through. Some of the best sentences are those describing the work of the gypsy, Fuentes:

> Alone in the center of the ring the bull STOOD, *still fixed.* FUENTES, *tall, flatbacked,* WALKING *toward him arrogantly, his arms spread out, the two slim, red sticks, one in each hand, held by the fingers, points straight forward.*

The second sentence has no predicate verb; grammatically it is an absolute phrase. *Tall* and *flat-backed* go with the subject, *Fuentes,* describing appearance rather than behavior, the first by quality, the second by detail. As a headword, *walking* takes the adverb *arrogantly* and the two absolute phrases describing the position of his arms and the way he holds the banderillos. The phrases *one in each hand* and *points straight forward,* both absolutes, modify *the two slim, red sticks held by the fingers;* these details within a detail represent a third level.

The next, relatively simple, sentence illustrates all three methods of description.

> The gypsy was walking out toward the bull again, WALKING *heel-and-toe, insultingly, like a ball-room dancer, the red shafts of the banderillos twitching with his walk.*

The second *walking* I take as in apposition to the first; it is a common practice to add an appositive noun or verb in order, as here, to separate the modifiers of manner from those of time and place, or to clear the narrative movement by keeping the subject and the verb free of modifiers. *Walking* is modified by quality in the adverb *insultingly*, by comparison in the *like* phrase, and by detail in the concluding absolute phrase; *heel-and-toe* is an adverbial noun describing by detail.

The next sentence is of a type, frequent especially in Hemingway's narratives of hunting, where the action involves two or more agents and the sentence focuses, by means of absolute phrases, first on one and then on another, with any number of third- or fourth- or fifth-level modifiers added to the absolute phrases. In this sentence, after winding the bull around himself like a belt, Manuel stepped clear,

> leaving the bull facing Zurito on the white horse, come up and planted firm, THE HORSE FACING THE BULL, its ears forward, its lips nervous, ZURITO, his hat over his eyes, LEANING FORWARD, the long pole sticking out before and behind in a sharp angle under his right arm, held halfway down, the triangular iron point facing the bull.

The absolutes in small capitals are subordinate to "Zurito on the white horse, come up and planted firm." The fear of the horse is described by two details in absolutes showing his alert ears and nervous lips, and the attitude of Zurito leaning forward by two more, showing the position of his hat and his pic. The last two phrases, a participle and an absolute, are fifth-level details picturing further the way he holds the pic. The five levels of structure in the part of the sentence I have quoted can be shown graphically as follows:

1 Zurito on the white horse,

2 come up and planted firm,
  3 the horse facing the bull,
    4 its ears forward,
    4 its lips nervous,
  3 Zurito, / , leaning forward,
    4 / his hat over his eyes
    4 the long pole sticking out . . . under his right arm,
     5 held halfway down,
     5 the triangular iron point facing the bull.

This, to conclude, is what I have found in working out Erskine's principle. The striking thing about this analysis is its simplicity. There are two steps in picturing an object or an action in words—naming it and describing it. (Naming has been taken for granted in this paper.) For describing either an object or an action there are three methods; and each method makes use of a limited set of grammatical constructions. These grammatical constructions are an invaluable clue to the sentence patterns of current descriptive-narrative writing.

The word *simplicity* tolls me back to the problem of teaching. Experience has proved to me that where the elements of descriptive-narrative writing are taught, an attack based on this analysis can produce results far beyond any based on conventional rhetoric—even with unpromising students, the kind who "skip the description" and whose critical perception and vocabulary are limited to the phrase "flowery adjectives." For, besides being simple, the method is specific, separating for study and yet correlating functionally the problems of observation, diction, and sentence pattern and movement and focusing on manageable units. This focusing on certain elements of style might be thought to lead to a patchwork, lacking integration and individuality, but in practice this is not the outcome. Because of the structural relations of the modifiers to the head-words, the person who is occupied for the moment only with the problem of making the particulars concrete learns insensibly a good deal about what particulars to present, and in what order and in what light.

It will be found that the three methods of description make different requisitions on the abilities of the writer —the first method, and also the choice of head-words, depends mainly on vocabulary, description by details mainly on observation, and description by comparison mainly on imagination. But the point of reference for all is observation, and the success of the instruction will depend more than on anything else on the rigor of the insistence that what is added be added from *immediate observation*.

But, of course, the teacher must first teach himself, just as in another department of our work the teacher brought up on prescriptive methods must teach himself to use procedures based on other methods.

❦❦❦❦❦❦❦❦❦❦❦❦❦❦❦❦❦❦❦❦

Sentence
Openers

Grammar and rhetoric are complementary, but their procedures and goals are quite different. Grammar maps out the possible; rhetoric narrows the possible down to the desirable or effective. The key question for rhetoric is how to know what is desirable. If we are not to inflict on our students our subjective impressions, we must look outside ourselves for standards—to authority or to the practice of professional writers.

The authority of the school tradition is so debased and unrealistic that it is hard to believe that it does not do more harm than good. One occasionally comes across a statement by someone whose judgment one can respect. On the topic of sentence openers, such a one as this by H. J. C. Grierson:

> English idiom has given the opening words of a sentence so generally to the subject that in many cases all we have to be sure of is that we have chosen the right subject of the sentence, the subject which the context requires. But greater freedom is left us in the choice of the closing adjunct. . . .
>
> *Rhetoric and English Composition*, p. 103

Or this by H. W. Fowler, on what he calls (2nd ed., p. 438) the "sentry participle, etc." in inch-long newspaper paragraphs:

> In these paragraphs, before we are allowed to enter, we are challenged by the sentry in the guise of a participle or some equivalent posted in advance to secure that our interview with the C. O. (or subject of the sentence) shall not take place without due ceremony.

But the opinions of those who happen to comment on a detail of style are no substitute for standards derived from study of the usage of those who make their livings and their reputations by writing. As much as anything else we who teach composition need scores of studies of details of style. And anyone can make such studies. It doesn't take a grant and it can be done without a computer. It only takes the desire to make the hours writing (and reading) themes a little less fruitless.

❧ ❧ ❧ ❧ ❧

The teacher of writing must be a judge of what is good and bad in writing. He must say to his students "Do this" and "Don't do that." In the United States there are said to be some 90,000 secondary teachers of English alone, and all of them are to some extent teachers of writing. What training have they had to insure that they are sound judges of what is good or bad? From what sources do they derive their standards for saying "Do this" or "Don't do that"? These are real questions and serious ones. It is not the purpose of this paper to answer them, but to report the search for a source for standards in one small area where the prevailing standards are more likely to result in bad writing than good.

The search started in a class in advanced expository writing. I had reached the point where I wanted to say something about sentence openings. I had a fine phrase to start with, "A sentence should have a clear head," and I was rattling along, saying "Don't start a sentence with this construction or that construction"—when a student broke in to say that in journalism he had been taught to use just such constructions and that he was rather fond of them. In such a case the proper thing, of course, is to say "In my class you do what I say and the school of journalism be damned." But I couldn't say that, because we had begun the semester with James B. McMillan's "A Philosophy of Language" (*College English,* November 1960), with its distinctions between subjective and objective truth and between grammar and usage and rhetoric, and I had said that any statements I would make about grammar and usage and, as far as possible (since it must still be classed as an art), about rhetoric would be objective and that I would try to label subjective statements as subjective. What I had just said about sentence openings I had labeled as subjective, as based on my general impression of the practice of professional writers. The upshot of the clash was the decision that the group itself could settle this question of standards by examining the practice of some of the writers in the two magazines we were using—*Harper's* and *The New Yorker*.

My *dos* and *don'ts* tallied very well with the practice of these writers. But the important point is that an admittedly hazy general impression was replaced by an objectively established standard—one valid as far as the sample was representative. From this start, I continued the effort to establish standards on the basis of actual practice—widening the sample enough to hope for validity. I have been rather surprised myself at what has turned up; I didn't suspect that the practice of experienced craftsmen in prose was so consistent and differed so widely from what we commonly teach.

Consider, for an example of what a teacher might take as providing a sound standard and an efficient method of bringing his students up to it, an article, "Variety in Sentence Structure: A Device," which appeared in *College English*, April 1950. The article offers a way to force to quick maturity the style of, let us say Susie, a college freshman, who, when allowed to write just what comes naturally, begins twelve to fifteen sentences in a theme of twenty with the subject and the rest with nothing more ambitious than adverbial modifiers. The device is a "sentence graph," which she is to turn in with each theme, showing the length of each sentence and the grammatical opening used. The instructor is to give a separate grade for the graph; his goal is to get something before the subject in 75–80% of the sentences, in the form of eight to ten different grammatical constructions. For, the author says, "When a student opens a sentence with an infinitive phrase or a past participle, we immediately stamp him as more mature in the sense of style than the average student." By this standard, it's what's up front that counts.

It ought to be easy to see the fallacy in this kind of teaching. Form is treated without reference to material or intent, and the prescription is the same regardless of subject or style—narrative or expository, simple or complex, informal or formal. Yet the validity of this notion of what constitutes maturity of style and especially the validity of the specific percentage of 75–80% are not apparent to casual inspection or reflection. But study of the practice of professional writers makes the fallacy painfully evident and provides a more reasonable goal for the teacher.

I have chosen for this study twenty recent or contemporary American writers—ten for narrative and ten for discursive writing. I do not pretend that they are the twenty *best* writers of contemporary American prose. Some were such obvious candidates that they could not be omitted; some were suggested by colleagues and students, some by reviewers praising their style; some were chosen to give a certain amount of variety to the sample. The reader can use my procedures on any writer he may prefer.

My samples were the first 200 sentences (except as noted below) from the selected work. A test with 500-sentence samples showed that they were not more valid than the shorter ones. Some types of sentences had to be omitted to arrive at the author's settled style: quotations and dialog and interior monolog as not being the author's style, sentence fragments, questions, and all sentences with "postponed subjects" (Then there were three / It is evident that / It is too early to say). Some initial conjunctions and adverbs produce inversion of subject and verb; such inversions were disregarded.

The grammatical constructions treated here as sentence openers are all (except as noted in the next paragraph) what Paul Roberts calls sentence modifiers (*English Sentences*, Chapters 19 and 23). They stand before the subject, but do not form a grammatical unit with it, whether the subject is a single word (*Then* he / *Then* Paul . . .) or the head of a noun phrase (*Then* all the ten little Indians . . .). The coordinating conjunctions (*and, but, or, nor, so, yet, for*) are not sentence modifiers, but they frequently stand between sentences: "*And* he . . ." was treated as beginning with the subject, "*And* then he . . ." as beginning with an adverb as sentence modifier. As will be seen below, such conjunctions were counted, because one of the four things every college freshman knows is that he must not begin a sentence with *and* or *but*. A sentence may have more than one modifier as opener—"*Then, long afterwards, when the old wounds had healed,* he . . ."; such an array was counted as one modifier, here an adverb.

The sentence openers fall into three sorts. (1) Adverbial. These may be clauses, prepositional phrases, adverbs, or nouns in an adverbial function (*Two by two,* they . . .). (2) Verbal groups. These may be present or past participles, infinitives, absolutes (*The really critical problems solved,* they . . .), or so-called gerund phrases (*After seeing his mother,* he . . .). (3) Inverted constructions. These include inverted appositive nouns or, more simply, noun clusters (*The mother of three children,* she . . .), inverted appositive adjectives or adjective clusters (*Angry at the long series of delays,* the men . . .), inverted progressive tense forms (*Waiting for fuller reports on unemployment* was the President), inverted passive voice forms (*Eliminated in the first round* was the Brazilian team), and inverted complements of several kinds (*More interesting than the sculpture* are the paintings / *What he wanted* he usually got / *The Brown Bomber* he used to be called). The last three constructions do not involve sentence modifiers, and they take more forms than I have illustrated; but they are sometimes recommended as devices for sentence variety and are frequent, especially the inverted verb phrases, in the practice of journalists.

One may use the following profile (62 : 56, 4, 2—18) to present the count for any given author. The number before the colon represents the total number of sentence openers in the 200-sentence sample; the three after the colon break this total down into the three sorts—adverbial, verbal, inverted. The number after the dash indicates the number of initial coordinate conjunctions. Any of these numbers divided by two gives a percentage. Here the results are tabulated.

Narrative	Sentence Openers	Adverbial	Verbal	Inverted	Co-ord. Conj.
Clark, *Ox-Bow Incident*	31	31	0	0	11
Faulkner, *Spotted Horses*	39	36	2	1	2
Hemingway, *Francis Macomber*	42	35	5	2	7
McCarthy, *Charmed Life*	38	35	2	1	23
Marquand, *Melville Goodwin*	29	27	2	0	0
O'Hara, *Ten North Frederick*	34	30	3	1	10
E. M. Roberts, *Time of Man*	45	42	3	0	2
Steinbeck, *Red Pony*	42	41	1	0	7
Welty, *Delta Wedding*	61	55	5	1	11
Warren, *All the King's Men*	39	38	1	0	18
Total	404	375	24	5	91
Percentage	20.20	18.75	1.20	0.25	4.55
Discursive					
Carson, *Sea Around Us*	79	74	4	1	29
M. Chute, *Shakespeare of London*	64	63	0	1	4
De Voto, *Easy Chair*	51	50	1	0	16
Edman, *Arts and the Man*	37	33	2	2	14
Highet, *Art of Teaching*	47	45	2	0	22
Mencken, *Vintage Mencken*	72	67	5	0	9
Lloyd & Warfel, *American English*	77	72	4	1	4
Trilling, *Liberal Imagination* (pp. 216-234)	60	57	3	0	34
Van Doren, *Shakespeare: Four Tragedies*	32	32	0	0	29
Wilson, *Literary Chronicle*: 1920-1950 (pp. 9-29, 422-427)	56	51	3	2	14
Total	575	544	23	8	175
Percentage	28.75	27.20	1.15	0.40	8.75
Combined Total	979	919	47	13	266
Combined Percentage	24.47	22.98	1.17	0.32	6.65

This attempt to test rhetorical pronouncements against the practice of professional writers shows that Susie, in her innocence, writes like the professionals. Like her, they place something before the subject in only a fourth of their sentences (24.47%), and, like her, they use almost nothing but adverbial modifiers. They use adverbial modifiers before 23 sentences in 100 (22.98%), but they use verbal groups before only one sentence in 85 (1.17%) and the inverted elements before only one in 300 (0.32%). Thus the only effect of the sentence graph would be to corrupt whatever feeling for style she had to begin with, to force her to write a contorted academic or journalistic prose—what might from its shape be called "pretzel prose." Unless we can do better than this, we might as well disband the class and go home.

For an example of pretzel prose take this article from a university student newspaper.

Europe Trip Slated by Professor

Busily preparing for his coming trip to France is Dr. Henry Makeweather, professor of French. (1)

Granted a sabbatical leave next semester, Professor Makeweather plans a tour of France, for further work on his dissertation, "A Dictionary of French Proverbs." (2)

Having written the dictionary for his Ph.D., Professor Makeweather will expand the work on this trip, adding proverbs that he hopes to find still in use by French peasants. (3)

"It will be very interesting to see the changes made since the war," he said, although admitting that transportation might prove a little difficult at first. (4)

This is not the first trip to France for the professor. He did graduate work for a year at the Sorbonne in 1932–33 and took a summer course in 1936. (5)

An alumnus of this university, Professor Makeweather graduated in 1928, having been president of the French club. A French major with a minor in political science, he was a charter member of the International Relations Club. (6)

Just a few of his affiliations are Phi Beta Kappa and Modern Language Association. (7)

Newly elected president of the Southern California branch of the Teachers of Modern Languages, he is also a member of the Men's Faculty Club. (8)

His M.A. was awarded in 1930 at Stanford. Before that time he taught in the San Francisco schools. In 1931 he began teaching at this university. (9)

Although born in Colorado, Professor Makeweather graduated from high school in San Francisco. (10)

"If I were starting over again, I would probably become a scholar," he said. "Proverbs have been very interesting to work with." (11)

This example does not quite meet the goal the sentence graph sets, since only 70% of the sentences (not counting the quoted ones, of course) have something before the subject and these involve only five different constructions. Even the deviser the the graph did not come up to his own standards. The profile for the article in *College English* (in percentages) is only 46.00 : 33.00, 13.00, 0.00. Indeed, I have never tested a piece of writing that did assay 75%. I must here begin to state subjective impressions and say that the closer any piece comes to that goal the worse it is stylistically. In short, the sentence graph provides a good clue to bad writing. The reader may check my subjective impression by comparing the stylistic effect of paragraphs 5, 9, and 10 and the quoted paragraphs with that of the other paragraphs about Professor Makeweather's trip.

The suggestion that we disband the class and go home is, of course, utopian, and I mean to be practical.

If we are to base our precepts on the practice of professional writers and if my sample is representative, we might discourage all of the five types of inversion as inappropriate to a natural style intent on conveying meaning and therefore unwilling to call attention to itself. The inverted verb phrases are the ones most likely to occur. They are common in less-than-top-flight journalism and in *Time-style*—"Running backward are the sentences until reeling is the mind." It is convenient for the sports announcer to start with the action (Scooping up the fumble and heading for the left sideline is . . .) while his spotter is getting the number (98) and identifying the player (Tom Harmon); but there is no such urgency at the typewriter. Paul Roberts (*English Sentences,* p. 154) says of inverted appositive noun clusters, "They suggest a formal and elaborate style." He might have said the same of inverted appositive adjective clusters. Their haunt and main region seems to be biographical notices and citations for honorary degrees. At the last commencement I attended, the fifty sentences of the five citations had nearly twice as many inverted appositives as the 4000 sentences of my sample—1 in 4 sentences compared with 1 in 300 sentences. Inverted complements seem to me less distorted, but of these James Sledd (*A Short Introduction to English Grammar,* p. 296) says, "Even in writing styles, tinkering with the commoner orders of subject, verbal, and complement strikes a good many readers as an extreme and somewhat crude device, which must have some special reason."

We might even try discouraging verbal groups as openers, except possibly gerund phrases, which I could just as well have counted as adverbial prepositional phrases. If the professionals average one such opener to eighty-five sentences (the highest frequency is in Mencken and Welty with one in forty sentences) and we find not four participles but *four dangling participles* in a theme of twenty sentences, then the real problem is not, as in all the handbooks, how to relate participle to subject but how to write without opening participles. The real problem is to undo the wrong teaching that has gone before.

This leaves us with adverbial elements as sentence openers. The natural function for an opener is to prepare the mind of the reader for the statement to follow. The adverb may owe some of the unusual freedom of position it enjoys in the English sentence, where nearly everything else is fixed, to the fact that adverbial ideas are often needed to set the stage for the sentence statement. Some adverbs (*again, moreover, in addition, ideally, in short*) are like the directional signs for traffic. These are best kept inconspicuous, the shorter the better, and may without much difference in effect be placed after the subject. Others carry the more explicit adverbial ideas of time, place, cause, condition, etc. Whether to place these before the subject or later in the sentence calls for judgment as to the effect. If we say "Before he came down for breakfast he read a set of themes," there is both an element of suspense (the mind holds the time idea unresolved until the act is indicated) and of preparation (when the act comes it comes invested with the time idea). If we change the order, the forward movement of the sentence stops after "He read a set of themes" and the mind doubles back and reconstructs the scene in the light of the time idea. Sometimes the intention is to force such reconstruction: "I will come tomorrow—if you want me to come." Sometimes, of course, rhythm or expedience determines the position; we have to put the modifier where it will sound well or where it will be clear.

Finally, a word about coordinating conjunctions as

links between sentences. In expository writing 8.75% and in narrative 4.55% of the sentences were so linked. In freshman writing, I should say, the accurate use of these sentence-linking conjunctions may be taken as a fairly good mark of a mature style.

The good teacher should not only base his preaching on the practice of professional writers, but should himself practice before he preaches. As Keats maintained, an axiom is not an axiom for a man until he has tested it on his pulses. Anyone who tries writing (as I have done here; the profile is 26.50 : 26.50, 0.00, 0.00–6.00) without verbal or inverted openers will soon find himself up against the traditional dictum about *and*-sentences. If he defies the dictum, he will still find himself in the company of the professionals—but this is a subject for another paper. Our trouble, as teachers, is that the approach to the sentence by way of traditional grammar (simple, complex, compound, compound-complex) and that by way of traditional rhetoric (loose, balanced, periodic) both leave us twisting pretzels. They aim to make one sentence grow where two grew before—"He stood on the sidewalk at the corner. A truck came by in the curb lane" becomes "Standing on the sidewalk at the corner, a truck came by in the curb lane." What we need is a rhetorical theory of the sentence that will not merely combine the ideas of primer sentences, but will *generate* new ideas. In such a rhetoric, sentence elements would not be managed arbitrarily for the sake of secondary concerns such as variety. They would be treated functionally and the variety—and its opposite, parallelism and balance—allowed to grow from the materials and the effort to communicate them to the reader.

A Generative Rhetoric of the Paragraph

It was just a hundred years ago, in 1866, that Alexander Bain introduced the paragraph into rhetoric as a unit of discourse. Bain based his definition and his rhetoric of the paragraph on an analogy with the sentence. This analogy, a very loose one, has prevailed for a hundred years. I have continued it—but with a difference. Here there is a precise structural analogy, not with just any sentence, but with the cumulative sentence. The topic sentence of a paragraph is analogous to the base clause of such a sentence, and the supporting sentences of a paragraph are analogous to the added levels of the sentence. The validity of the analogy is proved by the fact that a mere change of punctuation will convert some sentences into paragraphs and some paragraphs into sentences.

There are two values in this way of looking at the paragraph that I have not mentioned in the essay itself. It is a natural way to help students feel their way through the paragraphs they are writing and give them the density of texture, the solidity of specification, so many of them woefully lack. And in reading what they have come up with, a quick structural analysis will tell exactly what they have done or left undone, done well or poorly. Without such analysis, one cannot very well make any relevant comments. And such analysis is implicit in any sort of reading. After all, it merely raises to the level of a conscious operation what every competent reader does automatically as his eyes scan the lines of the page and what, I suspect, the incompetent reader has not learned to do. One has to recognize the shifting direction of movement and the shifting levels of generality. Following a paragraph is more like following a dance than a dash. The topic sentence draws a circle, and the rest of the paragraph is a pirouette within that circle.

This article was followed in ˜CCC by two others on the paragraph—by A. L. Becker, December 1965, and by Paul Rodgers, Jr., February 1966. The three authors joined with others in a Symposium on the Paragraph in the issue for May 1966. This symposium prompted the observations that I have transferred to a postscript.

❦❦❦❦❦

In my article "A Generative Rhetoric of the Sentence," I said that the principles used there in analyzing the sentence were no less applicable to the paragraph. My purpose here is to make good that claim, to show that the paragraph has, or may have, a structure as definable and traceable as that of the sentence and that it can be analyzed in the same way. In fact, since writing that paper, I have come to see that the parallel between sentence and paragraph is much closer than I suspected, so close, indeed, that as Josephine Miles put it (in a letter) the paragraph seems to be only a macro-sentence or meta-sentence.

The chapters on the paragraph in our textbooks are so nearly alike in conception that one could almost say that, apart from the examples, the only striking difference is in the choice of *indention* or *indentation*. The prescription is always the same: the writer should work out a topic sentence and then choose one of the so-called methods of paragraph development to substantiate it. The topic sentence may appear at the beginning or at the end of the paragraph or anywhere in between, or it may be merely "implied," a sort of ectoplasmic ghost hovering over the paragraph. Besides this, some books speak of "paragraph movement"—chronological (as in narrative), spatial (as in description), logical (as in discursive writing). If the movement is logical, it may be inductive or deductive or a combination of the two, and some books offer diagrams, as systems analysts use flow charts, to picture the thought funneling down from the topic sentence or down to it.

This prescription for writers and the analysis it is

based on are even more unworkable than the conventional treatment of the sentence as simple-compound-complex, with emphasis on the complex, or as loose-balanced-periodic, with emphasis on the periodic. I doubt that many of us write many paragraphs the way we require our charges to write them or that we could find many paragraphs that exemplify the methods of development or the patterns of movement.[1]

First, the methods of paragraph development. These methods are real, but they are simply methods of development—period. They are no more relevant to the paragraph than, on the short side, to the sentence or, on the long side, to a run of several paragraphs or to a paper as long as this or a chapter. They are the topics of classical rhetoric. They are the channels our minds naturally run in whether we are writing a sentence or a paragraph or planning a paper. There is no point in restricting a class (as for a whole semester in a freshman course I once taught) to a single method of development until the last week, when we reached what the textbook called a "combination of methods." It is almost impossible to write a paragraph without employing a combination of methods or to find paragraphs that do not.

In "A Lesson from Hemingway," I maintained that in representational (or narrative-descriptive) writing, where the aim is to *picture* actions and objects, there are only three methods of development, or description, as I called them, only three things one can do to present an image. These methods are to point to (1) a quality or attribute

[1] In this article I propose to deal only with the paragraphs of discursive writing and to exclude from these the short introductory and transitional and concluding paragraphs.

or to (2) a detail or (3) to make a comparison. A single sentence may exemplify all three: "The gypsy was walking out toward the bull again, walking heel-and-toe, insultingly, like a ballroom dancer, the red shafts of the banderillos twitching with his walk"—Hemingway. These methods are exactly parallel to the methods of development or support in discursive writing. The great difference is that in representational writing the methods are so few and in discursive writing so many. In either kind of writing the methods of description or development are hard to discern except in the light of what may be called a "structural analysis."

In the light of such a structural analysis, most paragraphs are like the sentences I called "cumulative." They exemplify the four principles proposed for the rhetoric of the sentence. Let us think of the topic sentence as parallel to the base clause of a sentence and the supporting sentences as parallel to the added sentence modifiers: clusters, absolutes, and nonrestrictive subordinate and relative clauses. (1) Then it is obvious that there could be no paragraphs without *addition*. (2) When a supporting sentence is added, both writer and reader must see the *direction of modification* or *direction of movement*. Discerning the direction is easier in the sentence because the sentence is self-contained and the elements added differ in form from the base clause. The direction of movement in the paragraph is explained below. The failure to see the relation of each upcoming sentence to what has gone before is probably one source of the difficulty many people have in reading. (3) When sentences are added to develop a topic or subtopic, they are usually at a lower *level of generality*—usually, but not always, because sometimes an added sentence is more general than the one it is added to. (4) Finally, the more sentences the writer adds, the denser the *texture*. The paragraphs our students write are likely to be as thin-textured as their sentences, and teachers can use this structural analysis of the paragraph to *generate* paragraphs of greater depth.

I have arranged the details of this approach to the paragraph under nine headings.

1/THE PARAGRAPH MAY BE DEFINED AS A SEQUENCE OF STRUCTURALLY RELATED SENTENCES.

By a sequence of structurally related sentences I mean a group of sentences related to one another by coordination and subordination. If the first sentence of a paragraph is the topic sentence, the second is quite likely to be a comment on it, a development of it, and therefore subordinate to it. The third sentence may be coordinate with the second sentence (as in this paragraph) or subordinate to it. The fourth sentence may be coordinate with either the second or third (or with both if they themselves are coordinate, as in this paragraph) or subordinate to the third. And so on. A sentence that is not coordinate with any sentence above it or subordinate to the next above it, breaks the sequence. The paragraph has begun to drift from its moorings, or the writer has unwittingly begun a new paragraph.

2/THE TOP SENTENCE OF THE SEQUENCE IS THE TOPIC SENTENCE.

The topic sentence is comparable to the base clause of a cumulative sentence. It is the sentence on which the others depend. It is the sentence whose assertion is supported or whose meaning is explicated or whose parts are detailed by the sentences added to it. In the examples that follow, it will always be marked 1, for the top level.

3/THE TOPIC SENTENCE IS NEARLY ALWAYS THE FIRST SENTENCE OF THE SEQUENCE.

The contrast between deductive and inductive, or between analytic and synthetic as it is sometimes put, seems to have led us to assume that the one kind of movement is as common as the other and that the topic sentence therefore is as likely to appear at the end as at the beginning. The many scores of paragraphs I have analyzed for this study do not bear out this assumption. Except as noted in point 7 below, the topic sentence occurs almost invariably at the beginning. In fact, I do not have clear-cut examples of topic sentences in the other theoretically possible positions. Readers may check their own actual practice and mine in this piece.

In connected writing, the topic sentence varies greatly in how explicit it is in designating the thesis of the paragraph. Sometimes it is quite explicit; sometimes it is a mere sign pointing to the turn the new paragraph is going to take. Sometimes it is the shortest sentence of the paragraph; sometimes it is not even a grammatically complete sentence. Sometimes it is a question. It seems to me that these differences are irrelevant, provided only that the reader gets the signal and the writer remembers the signal he has called.

4/SIMPLE SEQUENCES ARE OF TWO SORTS— COORDINATE AND SUBORDINATE.

Here the parallel between sentence and paragraph becomes fully evident. In analyzing the rhetoric of the sentence, I described what I called the two-level and the multilevel sentence. Here is an example of each and a paragraph exactly parallel in structure with each. The two sets of terms seem to me necessary to put the emphasis where it is needed in teaching and to avoid conflict with the use in grammar of *coordination* and *subordination*.

A. TWO-LEVEL SENTENCE

1 [Lincoln's] words still linger on the lips—
  2 eloquent and cunning, yes,
  2 vindictive and sarcastic in political debate,
  2 rippling and ribald in jokes,
  2 reverent in the half-formed utterance of prayer.

Alistair Cooke

A. COORDINATE SEQUENCE PARAGRAPH

1 This is the essence of the religious spirit—the sense of power, beauty, greatness, truth infinitely beyond one's own reach, but infinitely to be aspired to.
  2 It invests men with pride in a purpose and with humility in accomplishment.
  2 It is the source of all true tolerance, for in its light all men see other men as they see themselves, as being capable of being more than they are, and yet falling short, inevitably, of what they can imagine human opportunities to be.
  2 It is the supporter of human dignity and pride and the dissolver of vanity.
  2 And it is the very creator of the scientific spirit; for without the aspiration to understand and control the miracle of life, no man would have sweated in a laboratory or tortured his brain in the exquisite search after truth.

Dorothy Thompson

B. MULTILEVEL SENTENCE

1 A small Negro girl develops from the sheet of glare-
   frosted walk,
  2 walking barefooted,
    3 her brown legs striking and recoiling from the hot
      cement,
      4 her feet curling in,
        5 only the outer edges touching.

B. SUBORDINATE SEQUENCE PARAGRAPH

1 The process of learning is essential to our lives.
  2 All higher animals seek it deliberately.
    3 They are inquisitive and they experiment.
      4 An experiment is a sort of harmless trial run of some
        action which we shall have to make in the real
        world; and this, whether it is made in the labora-
        tory by scientists or by fox-cubs outside their
        earth.
      5 The scientist experiments and the cub plays;
        both are learning to correct their errors of judg-
          ment in a setting in which errors are not fatal.
      6 Perhaps this is what gives them both their air
        of happiness and freedom in these activities.
J. Bronowski, *The Common Sense of Science* (Vintage), p. 111.

The analytical procedure for discovering the structure
is really quite simple. There is no problem in locating
the base clause of a sentence, and one can assume—pro-
visionally (see 6 and 7 below)—that the first sentence of
a paragraph is the topic sentence. Then, going sentence
by sentence through the paragraph, one searches in the
sentences above for likenesses—that is, for evidences of
coordination. In both sets of two examples, the second
element is *unlike* the first one; it is different and so it is

set down as subordinate—that is, it is indented and numbered level 2. With the third element the two sets part company. In the examples marked A, the third element is *like* the second, it is parallel to the second, and' so it is set down as coordinate. The clearest mark of coordination is identity of structure at the beginning of the sentence. The fourth element is like both the second and third; and the fifth is like the second, third, and fourth. All the elements marked 2 have the same relation to one another; they are siblings. And because of this, they all have the same immediate relation to level 1, the base clause or topic sentence; they are all children of the same mother. In the examples marked B, on the other hand, the third element is *unlike* the second, and of course unlike the first; the fourth is unlike the third or any other above it, and so on. Search as you may, you will find no signs of parallelism. So, instead of two generations, there are five in the sentence and six in the paragraph. No element after the second is related immediately to level 1; it is related to it only through all of the intermediate generations.[2]

The fact that there are two kinds of sequences makes all the difference in what we can say about the paragraph.

It should be evident how we must treat the methods of development or support. In the coordinate sequence, all the coordinate sentences employ the *same* method—in paragraph A they enumerate the *results* or *effects*. In the subordinate sequence, every added sentence may, and likely will, employ a *different* method. There is no theoretic limit to the number of levels, and the lists of

[2] I use *generation* here metaphorically, in the biological sense, not in the sense of "levels generated."

methods in our textbooks are far from exhausting the whole range of what we may say in discursive writing to develop or support a topic.

It should be evident, also, that we need two separate sets of yardsticks for measuring such things as unity, coherence, and emphasis. Take coherence, for example. The repetition of structure in A is all that is necessary to join sentence to sentence at the same level. Any connectives other than the simple *and* for the last member would be an impertinence—*again, moreover, in the same vein, in addition* would be a hindrance rather than a help. But repetition of structure *is* necessary; like things in like ways is one of the imperatives of discursive writing. Any attempt to introduce variety in the sentence beginnings, by varying the pattern or by putting something before the subject, would be like trying to vary the columns of the Parthenon. In a subordinate sequence, just as clearly, repetition of structure must be avoided. Each added sentence, being different in the method of development, must be different in form. In a subordinate sequence, the problems of unity, coherence, and emphasis are altogether different—and more difficult.

Another paragraph will illustrate two other points. First, a writer sometimes intends a coordinate sequence but, like the dog that turns around once or twice before he settles down, takes, and sometimes wastes, a sentence or two before he begins his enumeration. (For other examples see paragraphs E and J.) Second, the coordinate sentences need not be identical in structure; they need only be like enough for the reader to place them. In this paragraph it is evident that all three sentences at level 3 present *examples*.

C. COORDINATE SEQUENCE

1 He [the native speaker] may, of course, speak a form of English that marks him as coming from a rural or an unread group.

   2 But if he doesn't mind being so marked, there's no reason why he should change.

      3 Samuel Johnson kept a Staffordshire burr in his speech all his life.

      3 In Burns's mouth the despised lowland Scots dialect served just as well as the "correct" English spoken by ten million of his southern contemporaries.

      3 Lincoln's vocabulary and his way of pronouncing certain words were sneered at by many better educated people at the time, but he seemed to be able to use the English language as effectively as his critics.

Bergen Evans, *Comfortable Words,* p. 6

*5/THE TWO SORTS OF SEQUENCE COMBINE
TO PRODUCE THE COMMONEST SORT—
THE MIXED SEQUENCE.*

Simple sequences, especially coordinate ones, are not common. More often than not, subordinate sentences are added to add depth to coordinate sequences, and co-ordinate sentences are added to emphasize points made in subordinate sequences. The resulting mixed sequences reveal their origin as derived from either coordinate or subordinate sequences.

My justification for the term *generative* lies here. The teacher can, with perfect naturalness, suggest the addition of subordinate sentences to clarify and of coordinate sentences to emphasize or to enumerate. With these additions the writer is not padding; he is putting himself imaginatively in the reader's place and anticipating his questions and resistances. He is learning to treat his subject home.

D. MIXED SEQUENCE—BASED ON COORDINATE SEQUENCE

1 The other [mode of thought] is the scientific method.
  2 It subjects the conclusions of reason to the arbitrament of hard fact to build an increasing body of tested knowledge.
  2 It refuses to ask questions that cannot be answered, and rejects such answers as cannot be provided except by Revelation.
  2 It discovers the relatedness of all things in the universe— of the motion of the moon to the influence of the earth and sun, of the nature of the organism to its environment, of human civilization to the conditions under which it is made.
  2 It introduces history into everything.
    3 Stars and scenery have their history, alike with plant species or human institutions, and
    nothing is intelligible without some knowledge of its past.
      4 As Whitehead has said, each event is the reflection or effect of every other event, past as well as present.
  2 It rejects dualism.
    3 The supernatural is in part the region of the natural that has not yet been understood, in part an invention of human fantasy, in part the unknowable.
    3 Body and soul are not separate entities, but two aspects of one organization, and
    Man is that portion of the universal world-stuff that has evolved until it is capable of rational and purposeful values.
      4 His place in the universe is to continue that evolution and to realize those values.

Julian Huxley, *Man in the Modern World* (Mentor),
pp. 146–47

This paragraph suggests careful calculation of what could be left to the reader and what must be made more explicit. Huxley took a chance on the first two items. What he added to the third made it a two-level sentence. The sentences he added to the last two made the paragraph a mixed one. He was under no obligation to expand all five items equally. The writer's guide is his own sense of what the reader must be told. In our classes we must work to develop this sense. The difference is often the difference between self-expression and communication.

E. MIXED SEQUENCE—BASED ON COORDINATE SEQUENCE

1 An obvious classification of meaning is that based on scope.
1 This is to say, meaning may be generalized (extended, widened) or it may be specialized (restricted, narrowed).
  2 When we increase the scope of a word, we reduce the elements of its contents.
    3 For instance *tail* (from OE *taegl*) in earlier times seems to have meant 'hairy caudal appendage, as of a horse.'
      4 When we eliminated the hairiness (or the horsiness) from the meaning, we increased its scope, so that in Modern English the word means simply 'caudal appendage.'
      4 The same thing has happened to Danish *hale*, earlier 'tail of a cow.'
        5 In course of time the cow was eliminated, and in present-day Danish the word means simply 'tail,' having undergone a semantic generalization precisely like that of the English word cited;
        the closely related Icelandic *hali* still keeps the cow in the picture.
    3 Similarly, a *mill* was earlier a place for making things by the process of grinding, that is, for making meal.

      4 The words *meal* and *mill* are themselves related, as
        one might guess from their similarity.
      5 A mill is now simply a place for making things:
        the grinding has been eliminated, so that we
        may speak of a woolen mill, a steel mill, or even
        a gin mill.
    3 The word *corn* earlier meant 'grain' and is in fact
      related to the word *grain.*
      4 It is still used in this general sense in England, as
        in the "Corn Laws," but specifically it may mean
        either oats (for animals) or wheat (for human
        beings).
      4 In American usage *corn* denotes maize, which is of
        course not at all what Keats meant in his "Ode
        to a Nightingale" when he described Ruth as
        standing "in tears amid the alien corn."
    3 The building in which corn, regardless of its meaning,
      is stored is called a barn.
      4 *Barn* earlier denoted a storehouse for barley; the
        word is in fact a compound of two Old English
        words, *bere* 'barley' and *aern* 'house.'
      5 By elimination of a part of its earlier content, the
        scope of this word has been extended to mean
        a storehouse for any kind of grain.
      5 American English has still further generalized by
        eliminating the grain, so that *barn* may mean
        also a place for housing livestock.

          Thomas Pyles, *The Origins and Development*
            of the English Language, pp. 306–307.

Here the development has proceeded so far that the
four coordinate sentences (level 3) have become in effect
subtopic sentences. The paragraph could be subdivided,
making them the topic sentences of a series of paragraphs. The long paragraph looks well on a book page;
the shorter paragraphs would look more palatable in

narrow newspaper columns. Either way, the effect would not be essentially different.

The problem of a reader tackling a long paragraph like this is to identify the coordinate sentences. He reads one 3rd-level sentence and then some sentences explaining it as an example of semantic generalization. He must be aware when he has come to the end of that explanation and must then shift his attention back to level 3. He must recognize the direction of movement. The first three 3rd-level sentences are easy to spot because like things have been put in like ways: the italicized words chosen as examples have been made the grammatical subject or apposed to the subject. But the opportunity to make a deft transition led the author to vary the pattern for the fourth. I have seen readers stumble at this point, and I have seen some make Danish *hale* parallel to the four English words.

F. MIXED SEQUENCE—BASED ON COORDINATE SEQUENCE

1 This is a point so frequently not understood that it needs some dwelling on.
  2 Consider how difficult it is to find a tenable argument that *thrown*, say, is intrinsically better than *throwed*.
  3 We can hardly say that the simple sound is better.
    4 For if it were, we would presumably also prefer *rown* to *rowed*, *hown* to *hoed*, *strown* to *strode*, and
    we don't.
  3 Nor can we argue convincingly that *throwed* should be avoided because it did not occur in earlier English.
    4 Many forms which occurred in earlier English cannot now be used.

  5 As we mentioned earlier, *holp* used to be the past
   tense form of *help; helped* was incorrect.
  5 But we could not now say "He holp me a good
   deal."
 2 As for "me and Jim," the statement that *I* should be used
  in the subject position begs the question.
  3 One can ask why *I* should be the subject form, and
  to this there is no answer.
   4 As a matter of fact, *you* was at one time the object
    form of the second person plural, *ye* being the
    subject form.
   4 But no one objects now to a sentence like "You
    were there."

Paul Roberts

I have included this paragraph to illustrate further the
kind of clues that mark coordination: at the first level 3,
we can hardly say: nor can we argue; at level 5, *used to
be: now;* at the second level 4, *was at one time: now.* At
level 2 there are no verbal clues; the reader just has to
recognize that "me and Jim" is another example like
"throwed" to illustrate the point that needs dwelling on.

G. MIXED SEQUENCE—BASED ON SUBORDINATE SEQUENCE

1 The purpose of science is to describe the world in an
 orderly scheme or language which will help us to look
 ahead.
 2 We want to forecast what we can of the future behaviour
  of the world;
  particularly we want to forecast how it would behave
   under several alternative actions of our own between
   which we are usually trying to choose.
 3 This is a very limited purpose.
  4 It has nothing whatever to do with bold generaliza-
   tions about the universal workings of cause and
   effect.

    4 It has nothing to do with cause and effect at all, or
       with any other special mechanism.
    4 Nothing in this purpose, which is to order the world
       as an aid to decision and action, implies that the
       order must be of one kind rather than another.
     5 The order is what we find to work, conveniently
       and instructively.
     5 It is not something we stipulate;
       it is not something we can dogmatise about.
     5 It is what we find;
       it is what we find useful.

J. Bronowski, *The Common Sense of Science*, pp. 70–71.

This would be a simple five-level sequence but for
the repetition at levels 4 and 5. It is a fair guess that the
desire for rhetorical emphasis generated these additions.
With five statements there could be five 5th-level sentences, but the author has chosen to put them in three
groups. This is a matter of paragraph punctuation (see
9 below).

H. MIXED SEQUENCE—BASED ON SUBORDINATE SEQUENCE

1 Science as we know it indeed is a creation of the last three
  hundred years.
  2 It has been made in and by the world that took its
    settled shape about 1660, when Europe at last shook
    off the long nightmare of religious wars and settled
    into a life of inquisitive trade and industry.
    3 Science is embodied in those new societies;
     it has been made by them and has helped to make
     them.
      4 The medieval world was passive and symbolic;
       it saw in the forms of nature the signatures of the
       Creator.
      4 From the first stirrings of science among the Italian
       merchant adventurers of the Renaissance, the
       modern world has been an active machine.

> 5 That world became the everyday world of trade in the seventeenth century, and
>> the interests were appropriately astronomy and the instruments of voyage, among them the magnet.
> 5 A hundred years later, at the Industrial Revolution, the interest shifted to the creation and use of power.
>> 6 This drive to extend the strength of man and what he can do in a day's work has remained our interest since.
>>> 7 In the last century it moved from steam to electricity.
>>> 7 Then in 1905, in that wonderful year when . . . he published papers which made outstanding advances in three different branches of physics, Einstein first wrote down the equations which suggested that matter and energy are interchangeable states.
>>> 7 Fifty years later, we command a reservoir of power in matter almost as large as the sun, which we now realize manufactures its heat for us in just this way, by the annihilation of its matter.
>
> J. Bronowski, *The Common Sense of Science*, pp. 97–98

Conventionally, the "movement" of this paragraph might be called chronological; but it is only roughly so— it leaps, and at levels 4, 5, and 7 it lingers. Note the marks of coordination: level 4, *the medieval . . . passive: the modern . . . active;* level 5, *the seventeenth century: a hundred years later;* level 7, depending on *since* at level 6, *in the last century: then in 1905: fifty years later.*

The first sentence at level 4 ("The medieval world . . .") is interesting because the topic sentence limits the time to "the last three hundred years." One could easily read

through levels 1–5 skipping "The medieval world..."
The sentence has been inserted—extralogically and ex-
tra-chronologically—in order to set up a contrast. Such
inserted sentences are fairly common and were at first
very puzzling to me. Occasionally, also, one encounters
and is puzzled by a parenthetic sentence. Such sentences
should be set off by parentheses, but all sentences so set
off are not extrasequential.

6/SOME PARAGRAPHS HAVE NO TOP, NO TOPIC, SENTENCE.

I. PARAGRAPH WITHOUT TOPIC SENTENCE

2 In Spain, where I saw him last, he looked profoundly
    Spanish.
  3 He might have passed for one of those confidential
      street dealers who earn their living selling spurious
      Parker pens in the cafés of Málaga or Valencia.
    4 Like them, he wore a faded chalk-striped shirt, a
        coat slung over his shoulders, a trim, dark mous-
        tache, and a sleazy, fat-cat smile.
    4 His walk, like theirs, was a raffish saunter, and
        everything about him seemed slept in, especially
        his hair, a nest of small, wet serpents.
  3 Had he been in Seville and his clothes been more
      formal, he could have been mistaken for a pampered
      elder son idling away a legacy in dribs and on
      drabs, the sort you see in windows along the Sierpes,
      apparently stuffed.
2 In Italy he looks Italian; in Greece, Greek:
  wherever he travels on the Mediterranean coast, Tennessee Williams takes on a protective colouring which
  melts him into his background, like a lizard on a rock.
2 In New York or London he seems out of place, and is
  best explained away as a retired bandit.
  3 Or a beach comber: shave the beard off any of the

self-portraits Gauguin painted in Tahiti, soften the
features a little, and you have a sleepy outcast face
that might well be Tennessee's.

Kenneth Tynan, *Curtains*, p. 266

The three sentences marked level 2 are clearly coordinate. But there is no superordinate sentence to umbrella them; that is, there is no level 1, no topic sentence. With paragraphs such as this the topic can usually be inferred from the preceding paragraph. But sometimes the topic sentence is actually part of the preceding paragraph, arbitrarily and illogically separated. Or, as in J, the preceding paragraph *is* the topic sentence; the two paragraphs of J constitute a single sequence. The basic pattern here is like that of C; but with the series of three examples disjoined, they stand alone in a paragraph that has no topic sentence. Paragraphs without topic sentences are always coordinate sequences, either simple or mixed.

J. TOPIC SENTENCE IN PRECEDING PARAGRAPH

1 The mystical artist always sees patterns.
2 The symbol, never quite real, tends to be expressed less
and less realistically, and as the reality becomes abstracted the pattern comes forward.
¶3 The wings on Blake's angels do not look like real
wings,
nor are they there because wings belong to angels.
4 They have been flattened, stylized, to provide a
curving pointed frame, the setting required by the
pattern of the composition.
3 In Hindoo art and its branches, stylization reaches its
height.
4 Human figures are stylized far beyond the point of
becoming a type;

　　　they too are made into patterns, schematic designs
　　　of the human body, an abstraction of humanity.
　3 In the case of an Eastern rug all desire to express any
　　　semblance of reality has gone.
　　4 Such a work of art is pure decoration.
　　　5 It is the expression of the artist's final withdrawal
　　　　from the visible world, essentially his denial of
　　　　the intellect.
　　Edith Hamilton, *The Greek Way* (Mentor), p. 33.

7/SOME PARAGRAPHS HAVE SENTENCES AT THE BEGINNING OR AT THE END THAT DO NOT BELONG TO THE SEQUENCE.

Occasionally a paragraph has one or more introductory
(I) or transitional (T) sentences before the sequence
begins. And occasionally one has a sentence or more
added after the sequence has run its course; that is, the
first of such sentences is not coordinate with any sentence above it or subordinate to the one next above it.
They are related to the sequence, but are not a part of
it; they form a conclusion or coda (C) or provide a transition (T) to what follows. To save space, I have quoted
only enough to establish that the sentences so marked
are extrasequential.

K. PARAGRAPH WITH INTRODUCTION

I1 If you are at the beach, and you take an old, dull, brown
　　penny and rub it hard for a minute or two with handfuls
　　of wet sand (dry sand is no good), the penny will come
　　out a bright gold color, looking as clean and new as the
　　day it was minted.
1 Now poetry has the same effect on words as wet sand on
　　pennies.
　2 In what seems an almost miraculous way, it brightens
　　up words that looked dull and ordinary.

3 Thus, poetry is perpetually 're-creating languages.'
4 It does this in several ways.
    5 . . . .

                    C. Day Lewis, *Poetry for You,* pp. 8–9.

Most of the examples of what I would call introductory sentences are like this in offering a comparison.
The comparison is not carried through the paragraph,
but is used only as a starter.

L. PARAGRAPH WITH TRANSITION

T1 So far I've been talking about some of the world-shapes
    out of which poetry is built.
T2 But images, metaphors, and similes are not the only
        things which may go to make the pattern of a poem.
1 There are meter and rhyme.
    2 You may be surprised that I have not put meter first,
        after talking so much about rhythm in the last chapter.
        3 Well, the fact is that poetry can be made without
            meter or rhyme. . . .
                    C. Day Lewis, *Poetry for You,* p. 33.

Transitions from paragraph to paragraph are ordinarily
embedded in the topic sentence, as a single word or a
phrase, a subordinate clause, or the first part of a compound sentence. But sometimes, as here, they take a full
sentence or more.

The first sentence of a paragraph may even be a major
transition. It may be the topic sentence of a series of
paragraphs or even the thesis sentence of an article.

M. PARAGRAPH WITH CONCLUSION

1 When we follow the growth of science, we come to under-
    stand how that movement has been probing for these
    unifying concepts.

    2 Look at the movement of biology since the days of Ray
        and Linnaeus: . . . .
    2 Look at chemistry, from Dalton's law. . . .
    2 Look at the march of physics to unity: . . .
      3 We have seen this lead to the creation of energy from
          matter; to a picture of space as closed but possibly
          expanding; and now . . . .
C1 Science is a process of creating new concepts which unify
    our understanding of the world, and
    the process is today bolder and more far-reaching, more
    triumphant even than at the great threshold of the
    Scientific Revolution.
    J. Bronowski, *The Common Sense of Science*, pp. 132–133.

Concluding sentences are rather rare, and some of
them, like this one, round off a sequence of paragraphs
rather than the one they are joined to. Such concluding
sentences are ordinarily at a higher level of generalization than the sentences they follow, and those who take
the most general sentence to be the topic sentence may
take them for topic sentences. They may say that the
paragraph has two topic sentences, fore and aft. The
practice of professional writers gives no support to the
classroom notion that the paragraph should end with a
"clincher."

8/SOME PARAGRAPHING IS ILLOGICAL.

N.

1 Rhymes, as you know, generally come at the end of lines.
    2 They are put there because it helps to create and make
      clear the musical pattern of the stanza:
      the ear learns to expect a rhyme, just as it expects a beat,
        at certain definite intervals, and
      it's pleased when it finds one there.

1 But you may get a rhyme in the middle of a line, too: and some poets are extremely skilful in making assonances and other sound-echoes all over a poem.

2 This is often done by the use of alliteration.

3 For example,

> I hear lake water lapping with low sounds by the shore.

¶4 Those three 'l's' make a pleasant liquid sound: the sound here, in fact, corresponds with the sense.

4 So it does in

> Dry clashed his armour in the icy caves,

where the hard 'c' of 'clashed' and 'caves' seems to dry one's mouth up when one speaks the line aloud.

C. Day Lewis, *Poetry for You*, pp. 35–36.

The two sentences marked 1 are clearly coordinate. One has to say, then, that the paragraph is compound (a reasonable solution; there are such paragraphs), or that the first two sentences are introductory or transitional, or that the paragraphing is simply illogical, breaking up a short sequence.

Paragraphing at level 4 is even more illogical. It breaks up a sequence at the most unexpected point. Perhaps the tired teacher will sigh "If gold rusts. . . ."

On the other hand, many a run of four or five paragraphs totaling 500–600 words can be analyzed as a single sequence, with the paragraph divisions coming logically at the subtopic sentences. This is the consummation we should work for.

9/PUNCTUATION SHOULD BE BY THE PARAGRAPH, NOT BY THE SENTENCE.

O.

1 This brings me to the third failing of eighteenth century science, which I find most interesting.

   2 A science which orders its thought too early is stifled.

   3 For example, the ideas of the Epicureans about atoms
      two thousand years ago were quite reasonable; but
      they did only harm to a physics which could not
      measure temperature and pressure and learn the
      the simpler laws which relate them.

   3 Or again, the hope of the medieval alchemists that the
      elements might be changed was not as fanciful as
      we once thought.

    4 But it was merely damaging to a chemistry which
       did not yet understand the composition of water
       and common salt.

    J. Bronowski, *The Common Sense of Science*, p. 47.

This is a minor example of punctuating without an eye to the paragraph as a whole. The two sets at level 3 are the same in intent and, except for the punctuation, the same in form. Likes have been put in unlike ways.

Paragraph punctuation usually involves the choice of whether to make compound sentences or not. In paragraph G the same author wisely grouped five coordinate statements into three sentences, sorting them out on the basis of content. Paragraph E does not really have two topic sentences, and a semicolon would avoid that appearance. I have taken it as a rule that a sentence that merely restates another is on the same level with it. If this is a bad rule, then all the numbers for level should be raised one. In paragraph P the effects of repetition and balance would be obscured if the sentences were not punctuated as compound.

P.

1 Nowhere, at no time, have there been five and a half years
   so alternately wondrous, compelling, swift and cruel.

  2 As the Sixties began, our aspirant astronauts had yet to
    enter space;
    now, they practice giant steps to the moon.

2 Then, jet travel was a conversation piece;
   now, we change the flight if we've seen the movie.

2 Then, we were about to be swamped by a recessionary wave;
   now, riding history's highest flood of prosperity, we are revising our assumptions about the inevitability of ebbs in our economic life.

2 Then, our Negroes were still marshaling their forces;
   now, they have marshaled the conscience of mankind.

2 Then, we were arguing over the fitness of a Roman Catholic to be President;
   now, we subdue the nightmare of his murder.

2 Then, a Southerner in the White House seemed politically unthinkable;
   now, a Southerner builds with the most emphatic mandate we have ever bestowed.

2 Then, John Birch was an unknown soldier, actresses still wore clothes at work, and dancing was something a man and woman did together.

Leonard Gross, *Look,* 6/29/65

❧❧❧❧❧

POSTSCRIPT

In defining the paragraph, we encounter some of the same difficulties as in defining the word and the sentence. The natural impulse is to take as a word whatever lies between the white spaces in lines of print or script, as a sentence whatever lies between a capitalized word and a mark of end punctuation, and as a paragraph whatever lies between two indented sentences. But these typographic criteria are inadequate. Linguists have had to resort to what they call the phonologic word, and Mr. Kellog Hunt, in his study of the language growth of children, had to disregard their capitals and periods and take as a sentence what he called a T-unit, another definition based on phonologic criteria. Tagmemic grammarians are attempting a phonologic definition of the paragraph.

I have defined the paragraph as a sequence of structurally related sentences. Here structure is a matter of coordination and subordination. Coordination is often, and perhaps always ought to be, marked by identity or similarity of grammatical structure. Subordination is marked, but only vaguely, by difference. The difference is definite and clear within the sentence, where coordination and subordination are readily distinguishable. In the paragraph, as I have tried to demonstrate with paragraph F, we have to refer to the content to determine what goes with what.

My definition is useful as a description of the internal structure of any given paragraph, but it does not delimit the paragraph. Many a run of several paragraphs proves on analysis to be a single sequence. And this is as it should be; the 500 word theme may well be such a sequence. But a discourse of some length necessarily has introductory, transitional, and concluding material that does not strictly belong to any of the paragraphs that carry the burden of the discourse. These could, and perhaps should, be paragraphed separately, the frame separated from the framed. But we have come to expect the paragraphs of a piece to be of about the same length. So we run the frame into the framed, the way decorators paint the walls and trim the same color. This procedure accounts for the anomalies I have treated briefly in sections 7–8. Here is a summary, from the Symposium, of the analysis of a 600-word, 25-sentence, 5-paragraph summary of a dissertation.

The first sentence of each of the first two paragraphs might be taken as a topic sentence, but the first was the thesis sentence of the entire summary and the second the thesis sentence of the second of its two parts. If these structural sentences had been paragraphed separately, as would have been logical, what was left of each would have been a coordinate sequence without a topic sentence. The five subtopics of the second part were portioned out to three paragraphs—3, 1, 1. The controlling consideration here must have been physical; the paragraphs came out about of a length. The last paragraph was a conclusion.

Another observation concerns the topic sentence, a subject of much unwarranted abuse. A better term might be *lead sentence* or *thesis sentence*. I have used *topic* so that I could call it the *top* sentence of the sequence and describe it as the one the other sentences depend from, the one they develop or amplify, the one they are a comment on. This, I submit, is a better key to the structure of the paragraph than the common notion that the topic sentence is the most general or the most abstract sentence of the paragraph. It is difficult to gauge the relative generality or abstractness of the sentences of a paragraph, and the attempt to do so has led to finding topic sentences all up and down the paragraph—at beginning or end or between or at both ends. Many of these sentences are the extrasequential transitions or conclusions that I have described. But some are not; they are part of the sequence. In saying this, I have to give up the notion implicit in the principle of levels of generality that *each* sentence in a paragraph is less general or abstract than the one it is added to. The trend of the added sentences is toward the concrete and specific. In a coordinate sequence, the coordinate sentences are at the same level of generality, and the set is at a lower level than the topic sentence. But in a subordinate sequence one simply cannot maintain that each is at a lower level of generality than the one above it. This is another way of saying that the common notion of paragraph movement as deductive (most general sentence at the beginning) or inductive (most general sentence at the end) or a combination of the two (most general sentence at both ends or in the middle) is not fruitful, except of confusion.

**In
Defense
of the
Absolute**

As reprinted here, this article is a bit longer than the version that appeared in *College English* and *The English Journal* in May 1950. I have restored the cuts made to accommodate it to the two-page format of the Usage Forum.

It was vain, I suppose, to have hoped that all the foolish notions rife about the nature and effect of the absolute construction would be "snuffed out by an article."

Porter G. Perrin immediately rewrote the entry in his scholarly *Index* (and suggested the absolute to Margueritte Johnson as a dissertation topic), but textbooks still continue to appear that by their treatment of this construction prove that their authors do not attend to the relevant scholarship or read literature with any alertness to style.

In a postscript I have tried to clear up a misconception that is still prevalent about the grammatical character of the verbid clause, as Miss Johnson terms it—M. Margueritte Johnson (now Mrs. Caldwell), *The Verbid Clause in Current English*, unpublished dissertation, University of Washington, 1960.

A useful companion to this piece is one by my colleague Orin Seright—"On Defining the Appositive," *CCC*, May 1966. The appositive, though it has not been disparaged, has been treated with as little understanding as the absolute.

❦❦❦❦❦

This article will use the nominative absolute construction as a measure of how far the books that purport to teach us how to use our language, even some of the generally good ones, have to go if their grammatical information is to bear any useful relation to rhetoric—if it is to be functional in the sense of functioning in the analysis and practice of writing. The nominative absolute construction is a thoroughly established idiom, about of an age with the perfect and progressive verb forms; it is neat and terse in expository writing and indispensable in descriptive and narrative writing; and yet it is almost uniformly misrepresented and as a consequence of the misrepresentation abused and condemned.

Here are some of the hard words applied to the construction, arranged and labeled to show the particulars of the bill. Its origin: "un-English" (Sweet, *A New English Grammar,* Part II); "generally an alien air" (Fowler, *The King's English*); "not idiomatic" (Perrin, *A Guide and Index to English,* 1st ed.). Its present level: "uncolloquial" (Sweet); "somewhat literary" (Bryant, *A Functional English Grammar*); "almost altogether a literary construction" (Kennedy, *Current English*). Its grammatical character: "weak," "difficult to manage" (Ward, *What is English?*); "a syntactical shortcut of a somewhat noncommittal sort" (Kennedy); several (Kennedy, Ward, and Pence, *A Grammar of Present-Day English*) regard it as a source of error, apparently because they regard it as an introductory sentence element that may be confused with the participle and lead to dangling participles. Its stylistic effect: "stiff" (Ward); "usually awkward" (Perrin).

Five of these guides admonish us to avoid the construction: "not only uncolloquial, but . . . to be avoided in writing as well" (Sweet); "not much to be recommended . . . but it is sometimes useful" (Fowler; this warning is not repeated in *Modern English Usage*); "Students are rather fond of absolutes, and will grow fonder if given the least encouragement. They should rather be discouraged . . ." (Ward); "ungraceful in the hands of an inexpert writer" (Pence; repeated from his earlier *College Composition* and *Style Book*); "dangerous for the younger writer" (Kennedy).

It is true that these writers, if they were granted their examples, could make good their judgments. The trouble is that they would be describing the elephant by reference only to the tail. In their confected examples (quoted ones should be required in textbooks) the position of the absolute‑construction is nearly always before the governing clause and the grammatical relation implied is always time, cause, condition, or concession. The key to the defense of the absolute is that these uses are all but negligible. The major use is to add detail to the sentence, what is usually called in grammar "attendant circumstances," but to which Curme adds "manner" and Jespersen "descriptive details." For simplicity I would say that the major use is to add narrative details, picturing an action ("Ellen watched her receding, a large woman, *her skirt kicking out in little points at the hem as she* walked"/"An owl sang in a tree by a farm gate, *his notes coming in a low trill*" [E. M. Roberts]); descriptive details, static rather than active, picturing appearance rather than action ("Her eyes were quite wide, almost black, *the lamplight on her face and the tiny reflections of his face in her pupils like peas in two inkwells*" [Faulkner]); and, I think one has to add, explanatory details ("To yoke me as his yokefellow, *our crimes our common cause*" [Joyce]). Sometimes the absolute construction is introduced by the preposition, *with,* here an empty form word ("The bull, *with his tongue out, his barrel heaving,* was watching the gypsy" [Hemingway]). In these uses the absolute nearly always follows the governing clause, filling in details of the action, picture, or statement which the governing clause merely blocks out in general terms. But the effect is the same regardless of position; and the effect is not unidiomatic, formal, indefinite, or awkward.

This misrepresentation is not due to lack of adequate scholarship. The oldest book cited above is Sweet's, which came out in 1898. Five years before that C. H. Ross (*PMLA*, 1893) traced the establishment of the idiom in modern English and described its stylistic effect as giving the sentence "variety and compactness," "freedom and movement." Poutsma (*A Grammar of Late Modern English,* Part I, First Half, 2nd ed., 1928) and Curme (*Syntax,* 1931) handle the idiom adequately and accurately, both recognizing its use for attendant circumstances, both recognizing this as the most common and natural use, and both recognizing that the construction is often introduced by *with.* Curme says that it is "a terse and convenient construction for all practical purposes. For the most part, however, it has become better established in the literary language than in colloquial and popular speech." The most nearly popular and colloquial types he considers those with an adverb or prepositional phrase for the predicate ("He sat at the table, *collar off, head down,* and *pen in position*"). The type with *with* ("He sat at the table, *with collar off . . .*") he calls "native English." It was, he says, "common in Old English and the older stages of all the Germanic languages and is still everywhere in common use." Poutsma concurs in this evaluation of the type with *with:* "frequently met with, also in ordinary spoken language." Curme also recognizes that in popular speech, especially in Irish, the construction is sometimes introduced by *and* ("Did you not hear

his reverence, *and he speaking to you now?*" [Synge])
and that in this construction, as elsewhere in popular
speech, the nominative is often replaced by the accusative ("It will be a very good match for me, m'm, *me
being an orphan girl*" [Wells]).

Of the college-level grammars of the older sort, the
following are accurate and reasonably full on this point,
the best being the two by Curme: Curme, *College Eng-
lish Grammar* and *Principles and Practice of English
Grammar;* Jespersen, *Essentials of English Grammar,* and
Onions, *An Advanced English Syntax.* The best examples
I have seen, all quoted, are in a high school text, *A
Grammar of Living English,* by McKnight, Haber, and
Hatfield.

But if writers of textbooks do not attend to scholarship,
they must read fiction, and a few pages from almost any
piece of modern narrative writing would provide data for
determining the present status of the construction. For
illustration I have taken the four novels and stories from
which I have just cited examples. In 180 pages there are,
by my count, 440 absolute constructions, very close to
2 1/2 to the page, with as many as 10 or 11 to a single
page and as many as 5 in series in a single sentence.
They range in frequency from 88 in the first 50 pages of
Ulysses (Modern Library), 126 in the first 50 of Roberts's
The Time of Man (Viking), 79 in the 30 pages of Hemingway's *The Undefeated* (Modern Library), to 146 in the
first 50 of Faulkner's *Sanctuary* (Penguin). This makes
an average per page of 1.8, 2.5, 2.6, and 2.9.

Of the 440, only 1, indicating time, cannot be brought
readily under the categories of narrative, descriptive,
and explanatory details ("*The garment removed,* she

stood clothed . . ." [Roberts]). Only 9 stand before the governing clause. Several come within it. In one sentence, for a reason easy to infer, Hemingway has separated the four absolutes, placing two before and two after the main clause (*"Heads up,* swinging with the music, *their right arms swinging free,* they stepped out, crossing the sanded arena under the arclights, *the cuadrillas opening out behind, the picadors riding after"*).

The governing element need not be a clause. The absolute construction may be attached to almost anything —to a noun ("Then Henry's WAGON, a rough old thing mended everywhere, *her mother inside on the bed, herself driving the team, her father bringing up the horses"* [Roberts]), an infinitive ("TO YOKE me as his yokefellow, *our crimes our common cause"* [Joyce]), a participle ("CROUCHING by a patient cow at daybreak in the lush fields, a witch on her toadstool, *her wrinkled fingers quick at the squirting dugs"* [Joyce]), or another absolute ("PARIS RAWLY WAKING, *crude sunlight on her lemon streets"* [Joyce]), or to nothing at all. There are 5 absolutes punctuated as sentences in Hemingway, 20 in Joyce, and 29 in Roberts. In Hemingway and Joyce they usually function as narrative sentences, but a few in Joyce are used for a kind of lyric refrain ("A tide westering, moondrawn, in her wake"). In Roberts they all occur in dialog or interior monolog ("Me a-comen down in the morning dew with a flower basket on my arm. Me a-cooken breakfast and a-setten out the pretties").

As to the grammatical character of the construction itself, the common descriptions are not quite accurate. It regularly consists of two parts, a subject and a predicate, either of which may be compound. The subject is usually a noun rather than a pronoun and therefore shows no case form. If a pronoun, it is usually nominative in standard English, though the accusative appears, as in Hemingway (". . . Wilson sat in the rear seat of the doorless, box-bodied motor car beside his wife, *them* both grinning with excitement . . ." *Short Happy Life of Francis Macomber*), and the accusative is common in popular speech. The expletive *there* may be used ("Locke states that, *there being no innate ideas,* knowledge must be won by active employment of our faculties" [J. V. Logan, *Wordsworthian Criticism*]), and no doubt *it* may be used, though I have to confect an example ("We left reluctantly, *it being clear that we could do nothing to help*"). The predicate does not necessarily have a verb. If there is a verb, it may be a participle, present or past, with or without complements, or it may, though this is rare, be an infinitive ("Meanwhile the cardinal is in jail, the sentence to be pronounced tomorrow" [Lowell Thomas, February 7, 1949]). Where there is no verb, the predicate may be an adjective ("She looked at him, her mouth boldly *scarlet*, her eyes *watchful* and *cold* beneath the brimless hat . . ." [Faulkner]), a noun ("As the bull lowered his head to hook, Fuentes leaned backward, his arms came together and rose, his two hands touching, the banderillos two red descending *lines*" [Hemingway]), a pronoun ("They ate the food in silence, the only sound *that* of the clicking knives and sweeping spoons" [Roberts, p. 64]), an adverb (". . . the horse facing the bull, its ears *forward*, its lips nervous . . ." [Hemingway]), a prepositional phrase ("Zurito sat there, his feet *in the box-stirrups,* his great legs in the buckskin-covered armor gripping the horse, the reins *in his left hand,* the long pic held in his right hand, his broad hat well *down over his eyes* to shade them from the lights, watching the distant door of the toril" [Hemingway]), or a comparison with *like* ("Across the child Temple gazed at the woman's back, her face *like a small pale mask beneath the precarious hat*" [Faulkner]) or with *as (. . . as)* ("The woman watched her, her face motionless, *as rigid as when she had been speaking*" [Faulkner]). Occasionally subject and predicate are inverted ("*Moving* through the air high *spars* of a threemaster, her sails brailed up on the crosstrees, homing, upstream, silent moving, a silent ship" [Joyce]).

The loose way in which the absolute construction is related to the rest of the sentence, instead of being a weakness as Kennedy seems to feel, is one of its advantages, especially in descriptive-narrative writing. In modern English the typical sentence in this kind of writing is cumulative, the main clause merely a base to which to attach, not subordinate clauses with precise conjunctions, but loosely related appositives, prepositional phrases, participles, and absolutes. A second advantage of the absolute is that it requires no verb, always an asset when the sense calls for nothing more than a copula. A third advantage is that it has a subject of its own, whereas the participle, with which it shares the main burden of carrying details, must take its subject from the governing element. The advantage of being able to notice the parts separately from the whole can be seen in the two long sentences already quoted from Hemingway, where absolutes and participles are used in series, and in a sentence such as this: "She jumped from her seat and ran up the banks of the ravine, terrified, clutching at the brush, dry stones rattling back in her path" (Roberts).

So far I have offered only isolated sentences. To illustrate the construction in context one could use a passage that George Mayberry chose for analysis a few years ago (*New Republic*, 100:608, May 1, 1944) because of the "clean-limbed functional quality of the prose," prose, he says, "that superbly fulfills its function; here of rendering the color, pageantry, and above all the movement of a circus performance as it works upon a boy's imagination." The boy is Huck Finn and the book is the fountainhead of the colloquial tradition in American literature.

It was a real bully circus. It was the splendidest sight that ever was when they all COME RIDING IN, two and two, and gentleman and lady, side by side, *the men just in their drawers and undershirts, and no shoes nor stirrups, and resting their hands on their thighs easy and comfortable*—there must 'a' been twenty of them—and *every lady with a lovely complexion, and perfectly beautiful, and looking just like a gang of real sure-enough queens, and dressed in clothes that cost millions of dollars, and just littered with diamonds.* It was a powerful fine sight; I never see anything so lovely. And then one by one they got up and stood, and WENT A-WEAVING around the ring so gentle and wavy and graceful, *the men looking ever so tall and airy and straight, with their heads bobbing and skimming along away up there under the tent-roof,* and *every lady's rose-leafy dress flapping soft and silky around her hips,* and *she looking like the most loveliest parasol.*
    And then faster and faster they WENT, *all of them danc-*

ing, first one foot stuck out in the air and then the other, the horses leaning more and more, and *the ringmaster going round and round the center pole, cracking his whip and shouting "Hi!—hi!"* and *the clown cracking jokes behind him;* and by and by all hands dropped the reins and every lady put her knuckles on her hips and every gentleman folded his arms, and then how the horses did lean over and hump themselves! And so one after the other they all skipped off into the ring and made the sweetest bow I ever see and then scampered out, and everybody clapped their hands and went just about wild.

❦❦❦❦❦

POSTSCRIPT

The two parts of the absolute are often (as by Margaret Bryant, W. Nelson Francis, Paul Roberts, and James Sledd) described as nominal plus modifier. This would make the absolute simply a noun phrase. If it were simply a noun phrase, the modifier could be expanded to a relative clause. In none of the absolutes quoted in this paper can the second part be expanded to a relative clause. If it could, *the resultant noun phrase would have no syntactic function.* If the two parts are subject and predicate, as I have asserted, the absolute can be expanded to a sentence. All of the absolutes quoted in this paper can be converted to sentences. If the writers had not had the absolute in their syntactic repertories, they would have had to put the details in separate sentences or phrases as I have shown by an example in the essay on Hemingway.

Conversely, a sentence of any predicate pattern whatsoever can be transformed into an absolute simply by changing the verb from finite to nonfinite—that is, by deleting the person and tense markers. If the verb of the sentence is a copula or such a verb as *seem* or *become* or a passive form, it is likely to appear redundant in the absolute and is commonly deleted. What is left of the predicate after deletion of the verb is the predicate of the absolute.

The term *absolute* itself is a source of confusion. It is used for constructions other than "nominative absolutes" and of the latter Perrin (4th ed.) says "They are 'absolute' not because they are independent but because they lack connectives defining their relation to other sentence elements, being joined to the rest of the sentence only by their position, by contact." *Absolute phrase* is doubly confusing. Miss Johnson's term "verbid clause" avoids both sources of confusion.

But another source of difficulty remains. Verbid clauses are not only sentence modifiers; they may have other functions. In such a sentence as this by Steinbeck (They . . . saw the quail eating with the chickens"), *the quail eating with the chickens* may be a verbid clause, object of *watched*, the equivalent, except for tense, of the infinitive with subject, "saw the quail *eat* with the chickens." But *quail* alone could be the object of *watched* and *eating with the chickens* not a predicate but a restrictive modifier, equivalent to *which were eating with the chickens*. Even in context, the sentence is ambiguous.

In the essay on the rhetoric of the sentence, the 3rd level elements of sentence 14 present a similar problem. I believe that they are verbid clauses—that is, structures of predication, not of modification. But in function they seem to be apposed to *sounds* in the base clause. Such are some of the problems we encounter when we try to pour the wine of living language into the bottles, new and old, of our various grammars.

Restrictive and Nonrestrictive Modifiers Again

This all-too-brief article has been included because punctuation—in speech, juncture—makes the difference between bound and free modifiers. Bound modifiers are restrictive; free modifiers are nonrestrictive. *Restrictive* and *nonrestrictive* are accurate terms and should suffice, but they seem to communicate almost nothing to our students. *Defining* and *commenting* sound better and may be more intelligible. Bound modifiers are defining; free modifiers are commenting.

Our textbooks are disappointing. Many of them restrict, and others seem to restrict, the discussion to relative clauses, and few give any more help in recognition than to say that the removal of the restrictive clause would "destroy the meaning of the sentence." None that I have seen gets to the root of the matter (Paul Roberts in *English Sentences* comes closest) by asking why we set off nonrestrictive or commenting elements. The root of the matter is that we set them off *to avoid unwanted implications.* A community newspaper ran on the front page accounts of two candidates for local offices, describing one as living with "his wife, Frances" and the other as living with "his wife Frances." I doubt that either candidate or that many voters noticed the implication of a plurality of wives, I doubt that the second one sued for defamation of character, and I don't know what a court would find, but it makes the world uncomfortable when we have to read men's minds rather than their prose.

I have inserted three new paragraphs into this article, and in a short postscript I have tried to relate restrictive-nonrestrictive punctuation to the other kinds.

❧❧❧❧❧

The article in the February 1957 *CE* by Wallace L. Anderson on recognizing restrictive adjective clauses is one of the many signs lately that things are getting better in the teaching of English. It shows what a difference it makes when the teacher is a scholar, competent in the linguistic disciplines relevant to his work.

But good as it is, it is limited. The problem of restrictive-nonrestrictive goes beyond adjective clauses; the principle applies to all adjectival modifiers, to appositives, and to some adverbial modifiers, at least to final adverbial clauses. Moreover, Mr. Anderson's third method, what he calls the pitch-pause method, the one he considers the most effective for most students and the one I am most happy to see adduced, is an oral method and is therefore limited generally to situations where the teacher can ask the student to read the sentence aloud.

But how does the teacher-as-reader know what sentences to ask the student to read? And does he have to accept the student's reading, even a halting one? Most of us do manage in speaking to get the junctures right, but how do we do it? And most of us English teachers can set straight the punctuation of a badly punctuated manuscript. For restrictive-nonrestrictive punctuation we usually find in the text clues to the *meaning*, and from the meaning, I suspect, we infer the junctures and from them the punctuation. But at times there are no such clues and hence either type of juncture is possible and either punctuation—but with a difference in meaning. What is this difference? The best way to frame the problem is to ask, *why do we set off nonrestrictive modifiers?* To answer this question is to carry out to its logical conclusion Mr. Anderson's second method.

Let me try to answer the question first by reference to some actual examples from my experience in editing. The book was bibliographical, the description of a valuable library. The author had written time and again that the library included "the first edition of 1672" or "the first Paris edition of 1672." This seemed to me ambiguous. Was the first edition of 1672 the *editio princeps* or the first of perhaps several to appear in 1672 with perhaps others in other years? Was the first Paris edition of 1672 (with what Mr. Anderson calls multiple modification) the *editio princeps,* or the first to appear in 1672, or merely the first to appear in Paris in 1672? Bibliography is an exact discipline; one doesn't want to set readers off on a wild-goose chase for phantom editions. Well, the author got the manuscript back with a query and returned it with the following forms: "the first edition (1672)" and "the first edition (Paris, 1672)." This is nonrestrictive punctuation and shows *the purpose of all nonrestrictive punctuation—to head off unwanted implications.* Conversely, *when the modifier is restrictive, the sentence makes one statement and implies its opposite; and what it implies is just as important as what it states.*

The contrast between restrictive and nonrestrictive is shown neatly by this example, involving appositives, in two sentences from one page of a book about Wordsworth, one referring to "his brother John," and the other to "his sister, Dorothy." One correctly implies that he had more than one brother; the other correctly avoids the implication that he had more than one sister. Without such facts at his command, neither speaker nor writer can manage his sentences correctly; without the same facts, neither hearer nor reader can question such sentences. Sometimes the only resort is to hedge. When my office didn't know the size of John Burroughs's family and didn't have time to ask the author or to check for ourselves, we had to change "Burroughs's son Julian" to "Julian, Burroughs's son."

The principle applies even to attributive adjectives— "There are certain words which some of us never use.

There are other, favorite, words which we are always using" (Edward Sapir, *Selected Writings,* p. 542). I have used nonrestrictive punctuation in the next example to indicate the junctures used by Howard K. Smith in a sequence of sentences in a radio report (2 Nov. 1952): ". . . two observations, one depressing, the other a subject for congratulation. The first, depressing, observation is. . . . The second, happy, observation is. . . ." Without the nonrestrictive juncture or punctuation, the hearer or reader would be alerted to look for more than one depressing and more than one happy observation. A class quickly noticed the anatomical absurdity of the pigeon they were asked to visualize as standing "on its favorite right foot."

The principle involved is equally clear with other adjectivals. Sir Ernest Gowers (*The Complete Plain Words,* p. 243) quotes from a manual, *Pre-aircrew English,* a wonderful example of punctuation gone awry with a relative clause—"Pilots, whose minds are dull, do not live long." The commas, he says, "convert a truism into an insult." Here the commas ward off an implication that is *wanted*—the implication that some pilots are not dull and that they have at least a chance to live long. A restrictive or defining modifier of such a plural term as *pilots* divides the class into two groups and makes an explicit statement about one group (the dull will die) and makes an implicit statement about the other group (the nondull will not die). What is implied is just as important as what is made explicit. Punctuation of such sentences turns on the question *all* or *some.* "Azaleas which are acid-loving do best in shade." Are *all* azaleas acid-loving and should *all* of them be given a shady location? If so, commas are needed to ward off the implication that there are azaleas that tolerate alkali and sun.

A wary writer, or one who read his sentences aloud, would not have sent these sentences to the printer without a comma each.

> "Robert Frost was the winner of four Pulitzer Prizes more than any other poet."
> "He had been one of two children born ten years after his brother."

What are the (probably unwanted) implications? How would one indicate that Frost won only four Pulitzer Prizes and not five, six, or seven and that "He" did not have a twin sister?

The verb clusters or phrases so prominent in cumulative sentences must be punctuated with care to separate the levels and make clear the doer of the action. Consider these four examples.

> "We drove through gardens dripping with shade and tangled flowering vines."   Fitzgerald.

It is the gardens that drip with shade. A comma before *dripping* would make *we* the subject of *dripping*.

> "He chased the old program, blowing gently across the green field, crossing one white stripe after another."

The comma before *blowing* makes *he* the subject of both *blowing* and *crossing*. With the comma removed, *program* becomes the subject of both.

> "He put out a thick, white hand bearing a masonic ring, haired over with fine reddish fuzz to the second knuckle-joints."   Faulkner.

The absence of a comma before *bearing* puts the ring on

the hand; the presence of the comma before *haired* puts
the hair on the hand and not on the ring.

> "Jackson men paraded the streets in the glare of torches,
> singing campaign songs, carrying hickory poles, gathering
> around huge bonfires blazing high into the night."
>
> Arthur Schlesinger, Jr.

The presence of the comma before *singing* makes *Jackson men* the subject of *singing, carrying,* and *building.*
The absence of a comma before *blazing* makes *bonfire*
its subject; a comma would throw *blazing* into the series
of verb phrases and the Jackson men would be blazing.
These commas are called the throw-back comma. They
are common but seldom commented on.

Quotations and quoted titles are usually managed accurately in speech but often are not in writing: "Hemingway's novel, *The Old Man and the Sea*" or "Hemingway's
last novel *The Old Man and the Sea.*" The first makes
The Old Man and the Sea Hemingway's only novel and
the second makes *The Old Man and the Sea* the title of
more than one of his novels. I was asked once to arbitrate
a dispute between an author and a publisher's reader
over the punctuation of appositive quoted sentences.
One wanted them all marked as restrictive, the other as
nonrestrictive. There were about as many of one as the
other, and each had to be considered separately. Here
is an example of the nonrestrictive: "Thus far, then, it
would seem that the question 'What is the realest real?'
is of no great practical importance."

Final adverbial clauses are hardest to apply the principle to, but this only means, it seems to me, that the
implications are not particularly evident or important.
Sometimes other considerations prevail. Here, for ex-

ample, a clause that logically seems to be restrictive can be read, punctuated as it is, as if the author were daring the deans to try: "I am pleading for such a policy in every dean's office. There are hundreds of deans who would quake for their academic lives, if they were now to pursue it."

Some of these distinctions may seem trivial, but they are distinctions we make habitually in speech. Our impatience with them in writing is a gauge of how much more difficult and self-conscious writing is.

❧❧❧❧❧

POSTSCRIPT

The textbook or dictionary that presents punctuation mark by mark—uses of the period, the comma, etc.—is of little use to the student working on a paper. He is seldom, if ever, concerned about the many uses of the comma. In writing or revising a sentence, he wants to know whether punctuation is required at a specific juncture and if so what is customary and acceptable. The treatment of punctuation should identify the situations that require punctuation and describe the options.

Most punctuation within the sentence can be described as structural. Its purpose is to tell the reader something about the structure of the sentence as a clue to use in reading the sentence. It attempts, however, to show only *three* things about the structure. To teach these three things and the marks available for each is a truly functional approach to punctuation. For each of the three situations there are three options. One of these may be taken as normal, but by choosing a lighter or heavier mark or a neutral or expressive one, the writer can exercise his own judgment and express his rhetorical intention. The choice of one of the three may be called weighting.

What follows identifies the three situations and the options.

A. A SINGLE MARK TO *SEPARATE* COORDINATE ELEMENTS

Three options are available, the semicolon, comma, and no punctuation (i.e., zero). These differ only in degree. (The colon was formerly used as a separator, a strong separator, as the word *semicolon* suggests.) Since independent clauses are punctuated more heavily than lesser coordinate elements, the writer must first distinguish between independent clauses and such lesser coordinate elements. And since the choice of a mark depends on whether or not the coordinate elements are joined by one of the coordinators, he must know these coordinators.

For main clauses the coordinators are *and, but, or, nor,* and *for, yet,* and *so.* (If the clauses are joined by a sentence connector, or conjunctive adverb *(hence, however, therefore,* etc.), they are punctuated as if there were no conjunction at all.)

For lesser coordinate elements the coordinators are *and, but, or,* and *nor.*

When the nature of the coordinate elements and the presence or absence of coordinators have been noted, the mark can be chosen by reference to the following scheme: *and* stands for any of the coordinators and A B C and a b c for any series of three or more parts.

1. Independent clauses

A; B A; B; C	Use of a comma constitutes a comma splice
A, and B	No punctuation if clauses are short; semicolon if they are long or contain commas

Treat all parts of a series alike unless two parts are balanced against another as in
A; but B, and C
A, and B; but C

A, B, and C A, and B, and C	Semicolons if clauses are long or contain commas

2. Less than independent clauses

a, b a and b	Comma if the two parts are long or contrasted, as often with *but*

Treat all parts of a series alike; semicolons if parts contain commas

a, b, c, a, b, and c	Same as independent clauses
a and b and c	Commas optional

B. A PAIR OF MARKS TO *SET OFF* PARENTHETIC, USUALLY SUBORDINATE, ELEMENTS

The grammatical basis of the sentence is the subject, verb, and complement. Because English has few inflectional endings, the order of these parts and of their essential, or bound, modifiers is relatively fixed. Any expression thrust between these parts or between any one of them and its bound modifiers is parenthetical. In reading a sentence, one "drops his voice" in order to bridge over the parenthetic element; and when he has bridged over it and picks up the thread of the sentence, he resumes his normal tone of voice. A writer must use punctuation—a pair of commas, dashes, or parentheses—to tell the reader which parts of the sentence he is to bridge over. And he must mark *both ends* of the parenthesis (the bridge must have *two* abutments), except that the first comma is omitted when the parenthetic element is at the beginning of the sentence and the second comma or dash when it is at the end.

The three marks used differ mainly in degree. The comma suffices for most parenthetic elements within the sentence, but stronger marks are needed if they contain commas or consist of complete sentences. Dashes tend to be expressive and to play up the parenthetic element, parentheses to be more formal and to play it down. Parentheses are required to set off sentences interpolated in a paragraph.

Some elements are always parenthetic and are simply punctuated by rule. Others are parenthetic only if they are nonrestrictive; they are punctuated according to the test for restrictive and nonrestrictive modifiers.

1. Punctuated by rule

    a. Mild interjections

        But she is in her grave, and, *oh,*
        The difference to me!

    b. Words used in direct address

        Now you have seen, *Henry,* what the consequences can be.

    c. Titles and academic degrees placed after the name

        John H. Williams, *LL.D.,* has been appointed director.

        Henry M. Wriston, *president of Brown University,* will speak.

    d. Items added after the first in dates, addresses, and geographic designations

        May 16, *1892,* is the date of his birth.

A letter addressed to 2432 East College Street, *Springfield, Massachusetts,* failed to reach him.

e. *Yes, no,* and (as used colloquially) *now, well, why*

Well, that is a different matter.

f. Idiomatic repetitions of a question

We are going, *aren't we?* He won't go, *will he?*

g. Minor sentence modifiers and transitional and directive expressions

This plan, *however,* proved unworkable.

The cost of electricity, *for example,* has gone down.

First, we have the wealth to provide these public services.

h. The speaker's tag in dialogue

"Don't you see," *he said,* "that it means trouble?"

i. Absolute phrases

He chuckled softly, *wrinkles forming at the corners of* his eyes.

j. Appositive adjectives—that is, adjectives placed after the noun

In this old house, *drab, ugly, and cold,* I lived two years.

k. Suspended coordinate elements

We try to live by the spirit, *not the letter,* of the law.

Skiing is an exhilarating, *but on some runs a dangerous,* sport.

l. After *namely, viz., that is, i.e., e.g.,* etc., introducing an illustration or example.

There are two tense forms in English: *namely,* present and past.

m. Adverbial clauses and some adverbial phrases placed before or within the governing clause. (Those placed after the governing clause are set off if nonrestrictive; see B–2.)

If this condition is fulfilled, an agreement can be reached.

The uses of the comma, *since they are so many,* are not easy to master.

n. All strongly parenthetical or foreign elements thrust into the sentence. (These, because they are usually longer, more important, and more emphatically parenthetical, are usually set off with dashes or parentheses.)

Against such men as Stevens—*and sneeringly opposed and repudiated by him*—stood the spirit of Abraham Lincoln.

A corporation usually prefers (*for excellent reasons, which we cannot now examine*) to have its capital account in stocks.

2. Punctuated by the test for restrictive and nonrestrictive modifiers. The nonrestrictive are set off; the restrictive, since they are not parenthetic but essential and hence are not bridged over in reading, are not set off. These, of course, form the principal class of free modifiers.

a. Adjectival (or relative) clauses, participial phrases, and occasionally prepositional phrases and attributive adjectives.

b. Appositives. (When an appositive within a clause is a series containing commas, it is often set off with dashes. When it comes at the end of the sentence and is formally introduced, it is separated from the introducer by a colon; see C.)

c. Adverbial clauses placed after the governing clause and occasionally adverbial phrases.

(Adverbial clauses placed elsewhere are set
off by rule; see B–1–m.)

C. A SINGLE MARK AFTER AN INTRODUCTORY
STATEMENT TO *ANTICIPATE* THE PART IT INTRODUCES

As used here, "introductory statement" does not mean
a phrase or subordinate clause placed before the main
clause (see B–1–m), but a grammatically complete statement used to introduce a statement, a series, or a quota-
tion. The part introduced is usually in apposition to some
word in the introductory sentence.

The three marks are colon, dash, and comma. They
differ primarily in degree, but the colon is markedly
formal and the dash tends to be expressive.

> We chose to read two of Lewis's novels, *Main Street* and
> *Babbitt*.
> It was a summer of pleasant diversions—swimming, riding,
> and dancing.
> Each piece is subjected to the following tests: chemical,
> mechanical, and X-ray.

Learning punctuation should keep step with growth
in syntactic sophistication. The cumulative sentence provides an ideal context. A single sentence may provide
all three situations. I have used the letters and numbers
of the above outline to analyze the punctuation of three
sentences on pp. 11–12. Sometimes a mark has two functions, as shown.

12

C   B2
We all live in two realities: one of seeming fixity, with
A2   A2   A2
institutions, dogmas, rules of punctuation, and rou-
B2
tines, the calendared and clockwise world of all but
A2
futile round on round; and one of whirling and flying
A2   A2   B2
electrons, dreams, and possibilities, behind the clock.

13

B1   B1
It was as though someone, somewhere, had touched
A1
a lever and shifted gears, and the hospital was set for
B1   B1–B1
night running, smooth and silent, its normal clatter and
A2
hum muffled, the only sounds heard in the whitewalled
C
room distant and unreal: a low hum of voices from the
B2   B2–A2
nurses' desk, quickly stifled, the soft squish of rubber-
A2
soled shoes on the tiled corridor, starched white cloth
A2 B1 B1
rustling against itself, and, outside, the lonesome whine
A2
of wind in the country night and the Kansas dust beating the window.

14

B1
The beach sounds are jazzy, percussion fixing the
C   A2
mode—the surf cracking and booming in the distance, a

little   nearer   dropped   bar-bells   clanking,   steel   gym
   B2   B2   A2

rings, flung together, ringing, palm fronds rustling above
   B2   B2–A2

me, like steel brushes washing over a snare drum, troupes

of   sandals   splatting   and   shuffling   on   the   sandy   ce-
        B1   B1

ment, their beat varying, syncopation emerging and dis-

appearing with changing paces.